Visions of H

A mix of memories, opi
and pictures by the people of Hastings

edited by Kay Green

'Rockpools at Hastings' by Vera M Vickers

Earlyworks Press

Visions of Hastings

Edited by Kay Green

Copyright Information

Printed in the UK
by MPG Books Group

ISBN 978-1-906451-26-4

Published by Earlyworks Press
Creative Media Centre,
45 Robertson St, Hastings,
Sussex TN34 1HL

email: services@earlyworkspress.co.uk

www.earlyworkspress.co.uk

Dedication

To the good ship Hastings
and all who sail in her

Editor's Introduction

This book grew out of a competition which grew out of an annual book fair. The first 'Books Born in Hastings' event was at the Jenny Lind in September/October 2008. It wasn't the first Earlyworks Press 'books and pictures' event but it was the year we thought of the title 'Books Born in Hastings'. The Jenny Lind celebrations included the launch of what was to be Terry Sorby's last book, 'Roadie & Co'. Terry was one of the founder members of the Earlyworks Press Writers' and Illustrators' club and it was his love of Hastings, and his energetic support of local creative talents, that shaped what we do locally. That same year we hosted a performance of Tom O'Brien's 'Down Bottle Alley', the play about Brian Charles Harding, and it was at the next year's 'Books Born in Hastings' that we had the conversation which led to the play's publication as a book, along with Tom's essay about Hastings' own 'Concrete King', creator of Bottle Alley.

ESCC Library display of locally written books 'Books Born in Hastings', Town Hall, 2009

The 2009 'Books Born in Hastings' was held at the Town Hall and included a fantastic display of 'live portrait painting' by Juliette Dodd and the results of our 'Visions of Hastings' writing and art competition. It wasn't easily to work out how to judge the competition. We'd asked for fact, fiction, poetry or artwork, from children, young adults and adults. We were looking for resonant, personal views of our town but the quality of each writer's or artist's craft and the originality of the result also needed to be taken into account. We found there were as many visions of Hastings as there were people offering views, and their talents were many and various. After much deliberation, the winner was Joyce Brewer. Her memoir of reactions to change spoke loud and clear about the mood of Hastings in particular and the more general concerns of those living in the 20th-21st century. Two of her pieces open this book, followed by Mary Horsfield's 'Hastings, this is Hastings – all Change', which took second prize in the competition. Mary's account of childhood holidays to Hastings shows just how much life has changed in a single generation, as well as reminding us of some of the things people will always love about Hastings. But this collection isn't all memories. Take Kristina Thurlow's 'A Past Eternity'. Is it a time-travel fantasy or a ghost story? Kristina is a young writer showing great promise, and her story, one of several weaving magic around the theme of the famous May Day weekend in Hastings, is included because it will strike a familiar note to many people. The poetry we received spanned many styles and forms; Joe Fearn, a well known local poet whose style encompasses mainstream contemporary and rap styles, put an unusual take on several local themes, making a striking contrast with Don Valentine's and Stanley Arber's more traditional styles in which they commemorate much loved aspects of Hastings' history.

Poet Joe Fearn entertains local writers at f-ish gallery, Robertson St, Hastings.

Joyce Brewer at 'Books Born in Hastings' Town Hall,
Oct 2009 photo © Victoria Seymour

We had been planning to produce an anthology collection of the winning works but the 'Visions of Hastings' file has grown since then. Our shortlisted writers sent in more works for us to choose from and those got us talking to other authors who had taken part in 'Books Born in Hastings' and more than a few of them had their own visions of Hastings to add to the mix so as well as a selection of work from the top twenty competition entrants, we have offerings from some well known experts on Hastings (that is, residents), who we chose for the interesting or unusual angles from which they could view the town.

Richard Pitcairn-Knowles with his family history display at 'Books born in Hastings', Town Hall, 2009 photo © Victoria Seymour

I am very pleased with the result and as well as presentation copies for all the contributors, I will be offering copies of the book to libraries, museums and local bookshops as I think it has a lot to say about the experience of our town in the 20th and 21st centuries. And last but not least, the book gave us a theme for 'Books Born in Hastings' 2010 – the launch party.

Kay Green, August 2010

Hastings Writers' Group and Ron Nicola's 'Millennium Chronicle of Hastings' at 'Books Born in Hastings' Town Hall, 2009 photo © Victoria Seymour

Anne Scott of the Old Hastings Preservation Society exhibits a range of local history titles at 'Books Born in Hastings' Town Hall, 2009 photo © Victoria Seymour

Contents

The Road

by Joyce Brewer

In 1935 Mum and Dad brought their four young children to live in Broomgrove Road, Hastings, in close proximity to the power station and Ore Railway Station. Parker Road was just being built and we lived virtually on the edge of the town, with farms and allotments our close neighbours.

The road was rough and unadopted, but as children we had happy, carefree lives; there was very little traffic so the road was our playground. The station and goods yard were a hive of activity, employing over a hundred staff, transporting thousands of passengers to London and Brighton and keeping the town supplied with coal.

Until the war started in 1939, life was good. Luckily, we all survived these harrowing six years. Then my two sisters and brother all got married and left home. My father then Mum died, and I stayed on alone in the same home. I retired from work. It was the same, rough road.

The old power station was replaced by a modern one, though never used – then set fire to in May 2000 and pulled down. The railway station and its sheds also disappeared and few people used the new halt, so the valley returned to its old self of flora and fauna, a real haven for lovers of nature.

Many attempts were made by property developers to build on the former allotments at the back of my house but nothing really happened until 2008 when one firm got permission to build 38 houses. But first they must make up the road to an 'adopted standard.' Men in hard hats came measuring up and so forth, and in 2009 the real work started. Since February it has been chaotic. Cables and wires have been accidentally cut and water mains hit: mud, dust and difficulty in driving to our homes; noise, vibration and not a clue about a completion date.

And when it does finally come to an end then they'll start on the houses up the back, which could take years rather than months, with lorries and diggers chewing up the tarmac road they have just put down.

And it's not a wide road, either – to keep down the costs – so what about on-street parking and two-way traffic? Not to mention our animals, trying to compete with vehicles on a fast new road that they've never been used to. To my knowledge, in all the years I've been here, we've never lost any pets or wildlife yet.

My green and pleasant valley, which I've loved so much, will be gone for ever: just another corner of Hastings under cement. People ask, "Aren't you glad there's a decent road, now?"

But after 74 years of managing without, I'm holding judgement, and my printable answer would be, "Absolutely not!"

New Residents of 'The Road'

2009 came and went – it is now 2010, and the road is still not complete. Traffic is using it and we all agree that what we've got so far is better for us and easier for travelling on, but we pity the lorry drivers having to negotiate their way down this silly little half-road and the walkers having to dodge the traffic which is where they should be – still no pavements: drains which haven't been christened yet; dusty, muddy and no sign of ever being of 'adopted standard'.

Yes, I'm still fed up with what they've left us with, but thank goodness for the wildlife that lives in Ore Valley, and has been visiting my part of Broomgrove Road since the 1980s. I wait until my neighbours have gone to bed, then feed the foxes and badgers from bowls outside my house. A couple of each turn up every night: not always the same ones of course, over the years, but their presence gives me pleasure, and they have become quite tame.

One late night in March of 2009, the moon hidden behind dark clouds and a gusty wind blowing things about, I'd fed the animals and gone to bed when looking out of the window, I saw these small, dark shapes skittering down the road but, feeling too tired, I fell asleep without investigating. The next night, in the light of a full moon, I saw what they were – four little fox cubs with Mum and Dad in attendance. I'd seen adults, yes, but not little ones in my road so you can imagine how thrilled I was.

This was the start of a unique period for me, just when I needed something to cheer me up, they appeared. But this was just the beginning. The following night, along came family number two. More cubs with Mum as nursemaid to join the first gang – it's difficult to count them when they're all milling around together. But hang on, we're not quite finished. Two grown-up badgers and four cubs came to join the throng. And if you won't credit what I say, then I have a neighbour who will back me up. Like me, he enjoys watcing wildlife but he's kept quiet about it in case the wrong type of people find out and harm them. And I do know that a police car stopped and tried to snap the foxes through their window once. They didn't succeed.

Anyway, we've now got everyone for lift-off, so let's continue; imagine being privileged to view fourteen or more wild animals gathered together and eating in one place. Foxes, badgers... and a hedgehog! Each night, after midnight, wet or fine, I'd go out with my big bowls of food, and there they would all be, waiting in a group, with the cubs getting tamer and bigger as weeks went by. I wondered how they all got into the den but of course, they had their own system and in their own language, told the youngsters when it was time to leave the nest. They were old enough to look after themselves, and find their own way in life and hopefully, be as lucky as Mum, and Dad and dodge the pitfalls of their lives.

They seemed to disappear so quckly from the road. One night here, the next, gone. I really did miss them. 'Vermin', somebody called them. Not for me they're not. They came to me when I was lonely, and answered my prayer. Thank you, my furry friends.

Photo © Joyce Brewer 2009

Hastings, This is Hastings – All Change

by Mary Horsfield

Photo © 1959 Mary Horsfield

I fell in love with Hastings at an early age. It was the happy holiday destination every summer for myself and my parents all through my childhood years. Leaving our small council house in SE London and travelling by train to the south coast for two weeks was the highlight of every summer.

The anticipation caused great excitement for me as a young child. I saved up my pocket money all year. I would have a new pair of white shoes and a new cotton summer frock made by my mother, who tried her best to incorporate my design ideas into the finished garment. Every so often, just before the holiday, I would take the shoes out and admire them, smelling their newness, in expectation of the dawning of that special day when I could finally wear them with the dress, and we would be on our way.

On a Sunday morning, Dad would sometimes bring me breakfast in bed and I would ask him to tell me the whole story of our holiday, just so I could re-live the previous ones and anticipate the next. I remember him mimicking the announcement on the train: "Hastings, this is Hastings – All change."

Mum and Dad packed all the necessaries, including a wad of notes (no cash machines then). Dad seemed to think we would suddenly be taken ill because we were going away, so into the suitcases would go various medicines, including chalky indigestion tablets which he encouraged me to suck "in case" I had tummy trouble. We always had brand new toothbrushes, flannels, toothpaste etc, which marked the sense of occasion.

During the train journey we viewed fields of sheep and cows (never seen in London), as my state of delirious expectancy grew ever stronger. There was always that magic moment when Dad would announce: "There! You can see the sea!" and I would scramble out of my seat to get a view.

The first thing I always noticed when we arrived at Hastings was the fresh air and the salty smell of the sea. The buses were not red as in London, but green and cream. I was also fascinated to see so many tall, white or cream houses, so unlike those at home. Many of them had a colourful curtain made of canvas strips over the front door, reminiscent of the stripy deckchairs on the beach; I always included these curtains when I drew seaside houses as a child.

We usually went straight to our boarding house in Braybrooke Terrace. The landlady was called Mrs Watson, and I thought she was the most wonderful person in the world (apart from my parents). She talked non-stop, laughed a lot, and told funny stories about her life as a landlady. She would always tell me how much I'd grown, and she would joke with me, calling me a "bobby-dazzler". When we left her house each day she would say, "See you later, alligator," and I would shout back, "In a while, crocodile."

Everything at the boarding house was different from home. There would always be a bowl and ewer on the dressing table in our room, and I have loved them ever since. But it was not just for decoration; Mum used to fill the jug with warm water, pour it into the bowl, and I would wash in it. More cosy than the bathroom!

Mrs Watson would bang a gong to call everyone down for meals, and there would be quiet, polite conversation in the dining room until the guests got to know each other a little bit. I was intrigued by the charming little decorated pots with tiny spoons to fit in a hole in the lid, which Mrs Watson used for her jams, marmalades and mustards. And she always warmed her plates.

One year, Mrs Watson's was unexpectedly full so we had to stay at another place right on the seafront. It wasn't quite as good but one advantage was the sea view, and that from our window we could watch the Guinness clock at the end of Robertson Street which played music every hour, and had little mechanical figures that came out and moved around.

Of course, my greatest joy was the beach. Mum and Dad would hire stripy deckchairs and read the paper. Sometimes we would brave the pebbles and paddle in the sea. Dad would look at boats through his binoculars. Woolworths' back entrance used to be open, brimming with brightly coloured beach paraphernalia, and I would choose a new bucket and spade. Mum would teach me how to pack the bucket tightly with sand before turning it over and patting it with the spade. I always longed to have a flag for the top of my sandcastles, but never did. I used to admire others' castles with battlements, turrets and moats that I never managed to achieve. Best of all was when the ice-cream man, with his white, peaked cap and deep suntan, came along, carrying his crate of goodies on his back. Mum would have a wafer or choc-ice, and I would have a lolly or cornet.

After a delicious lunch at Lyons Teashop would come the big question: was it hot enough to go to the open-air pool in St Leonards, which was my idea of heaven? If I got the thumbs up from my parents, I would be ecstatic with excitement. We would take the bus along the front and enter that enchanted place that afforded me my happiest childhood memories. It was there I learnt to swim, in my little blue elasticated costume, wearing my waterwings, taught by Mum and Dad. Each year I would be a little more adventurous, until I was swimming confidently, and even jumping off those high boards when I got older. After our swim, Dad would buy us all a hot chocolate and we would relax on those huge steps, covered in sun cream. This was all before the chalets were built. (We continued to go afterwards too, but the ambience was slightly less special then.)

When we left the pool we would often walk back along the seafront to Hastings, passing through Bottle Alley, which was quite elegant in those days. I was captivated by all those tiny pieces of glass in every shape, size and colour; I loved to choose my favourite panels.

Sometimes we would wander around the town going into gift shops, and Mum would buy kitsch ornaments or teatowels with "Hastings" on them for the neighbours who looked after our cats while we were away. I liked items covered in seashells, and the named mugs in The Rock Shop, still there today. Dad would take lots of photos of our holiday and get them developed in Marriots, also still there today. I liked posing for the photos and was very impatient for them to be ready.

We did not venture down to the Old Town end very often in those days, except for an occasional visit to The Smugglers' Caves, which really captured my imagination. There were some amusements on the seafront as there are today; you could ride on a small children's carousel, or put a penny in the slot in the hope that a miniature crane would pick up a shiny ring for you. I remember a small kiosk where you could put sixpence in the slot, make a recording of your voice, then play it back (no tape recorders then!) Mum and I did a duet. Sometimes we went on the motor boats which I was sometimes allowed to steer – that felt very grown up. Across the road were some bumper cars with rock and roll music blaring out, and I was in awe of the teenagers who flocked there.

After the evening meal at Mrs Watson's, we would often go to the pier. I loved the "Monte Carlo Rally", where you threw ping-pong balls into the mouths of moving geese to make your car race along the track. You could save up your winning tokens to claim a bigger prize if you wished. I was as pleased as punch one year when I won some plastic binoculars that looked a bit like Dad's. Or you could put pennies in the slots representing your favourite film stars: Fred Astaire, Ava Gardner or Marilyn Monroe, and if you hit the jackpot, a flood of pennies came your way, which you promptly and unwisely put back in the hope of winning again.

Tired after a long and enjoyable day, we would stop off at the milk bar along White Rock, where I would clamber up onto one of the high stools and drink a milkshake, while Mum and Dad had Horlicks. Then we would walk "home", admiring the coloured lights along the front, and the castle, which looked magical, all lit up in the dark.

Sometimes Mum and Dad would take me to a dance on the pier. They would do the waltz, quickstep, foxtrot or tango while I sat drinking 7-Up, which I thought was very grown up and better than squash. Sometimes, Dad would dance around with me so I wasn't left out.

We also went to see plays on the pier. I didn't really enjoy these because they were for adults and I could not follow the stories, so found them boring. But far worse were the variety shows where they invited children onto the stage to do a turn. I was terribly self-conscious and dreaded being asked. We also went to musicals at the White Rock Theatre; I loved the music and colourful costumes. The weather was nearly always sunny on our holidays, but if it did rain, I was taken to the ABC cinema to watch cartoons.

Those holidays were the happiest times of my childhood, but they must have made an impact also on my parents, because in 1977 they retired to Hastings, near St Helen's Wood. That was the same year that my first child was born, and the beginning of many more happy visits to Hastings, my two daughters experiencing some of the same delights as I had, and some new ones too, but with the added bonus of also visiting their dear grandparents. My children looked forward to The Okey Dokey Man at The White Rock, who sang songs and played games with the kids, giving parents a break. My older daughter always loved nature. I remember one particular walk in the woods on a Sunday morning when she was quite small. We suddenly came upon a field of ox-eye daisies, and her delight was clearly visible. Is it a coincidence that she called her first child "Daisy?"

During my childhood visits to the town, my mother used to explain to me that some people actually lived at the seaside all the time. I tried to imagine the joy of being in a wonderful place like Hastings and never having to go home, because it IS your home. I carried that thought with me all through my life, and the dream of living in Hastings never left me. Finally, by 2002, my parents had sadly both died, and my children had grown and flown the nest. I was at last in a position to realise my dream and move here.

I love Hastings for many reasons; it is a town full of character and with something for everyone. I cherish the memories that the town holds for me, and look forward to welcoming my grandchildren when they visit me here, and sharing in their joy. When I return to Hastings by train after a trip away, I always remember my father when I hear: "Hastings, This is Hastings – All change."

8

Pier Memories

by Angela Davis

Since becoming a Trustee of the Hastings Pier & White Rock Trust, I have been involved in tracing the history of the pier, not simply the architectural changes and changes of ownership that have occurred to the pier over its lifetime, but also the social history of the pier. It was during this activity that I came across a compelling photograph of a young girl, dressed in Edwardian clothes standing next to a very upright grandmother figure talking to a woman sitting on a bench outside the old pier pavilion.

Reproduced by kind permission of Hastings Museum & Art Gallery.

What caught my eye about the photograph was the fact that the young girl is laughing uproariously – very unusual for a photograph taken around the turn of the century. It struck me later that this young girl, had she been a resident of Hastings (and sadly I don't know her actual identity) would have witnessed most of the historic events that happened to the pier during her lifetime and so, my idea grew to develop a pier history seen through her eyes.

9

Here is her story:

I was very young when I had my first memories of the pier. My grandma used to take me on there on a Sunday for our afternoon walk in our Sunday best. We would stop and speak to people my grandma knew, and sit on the dolphin benches outside the grand pavilion at the end of the pier. My grandma especially liked Hastings Pier because they didn't charge you to promenade on it.

The Grand Pavilion had turrets with fancy ironwork and carvings. Grandma attended the opening of the pier by the Lord Warden of the Cinque Ports, Earl of Granville in the pouring rain on the first August Bank Holiday. He said it was a "peerless pier – a pier without a peer" it was also called a "Palace on the Sea" as it was so grand.

Eugenius Birch, the pier architect had worked in India on the Calcutta-Delhi railway. When he returned to England, he was asked to use his engineering skills to design piers and incorporated Indian-style turrets in his design. He designed fourteen piers in all.

Grandma told me that during the building of the Pier, a large iron pile for the new pier-head hit a hard object and broke the large screw. On investigation, they found a large oak tree trunk in the clay which was three foot at its widest, 24 feet long and weighed about two tons. Other similar tree trunks from an ancient forest were found during the construction.

Mr Birch nearly didn't see the pier completed, such were the disagreements between the directors of the Hastings Pier Company, the Glasgow-based Ironworks and himself. Delays occurred due to the wood for the deck being held up by the Franco-Prussian War, ironwork was delayed due to England having one of its worst winters – freezing the canals, stopping the transportation. Eugenius Birch tried to convince the Directors to build shops on the pier. This was refused initially, although they were built later.

People would spill out of the steamboats that docked at the pier. They had to extend the landing platform because it was so popular. Four steamboats could now dock together on the East and South side of the Pier-head. Once a new steamboat, called Rapid, ran aground on her maiden voyage from Eastbourne. People had to be rescued in small boats and brought ashore. The boat sat on a sandbank near the pier and we watched on the pier for hours until the tide came in and she managed to escape.

For a treat, my grandma took me to a show at the Pavilion. I remember gazing up at the ceiling and looking at the pillars and carvings. It was so beautiful. I can't remember anything about the show though.

Another clear memory I have is of going to watch the amazing Professor Reddish and his "Flying The Foam" act. He would ride a steep ramp off the back of the pier into the sea, much to the delight of the cheering crowds. It would be standing room only, the act was so popular. Sadly, Professor Reddish died during one attempt from Brighton West Pier.

People would fish from the platform at the back. New shops and a bowling alley appeared on the pier plus a building to house the Wheel of Joy. I remember this vividly, watching people sitting on this round disk that was spun at high speed – eventually flinging everyone off in a heap. We all roared with laughter as hats were

11

thrown off, and ladies ended up with all their petticoats showing when they landed.

When the Wheel of Joy was removed, the end closest to the promenade was widened. This was known as the Parade extension. Two new shelter buildings were built on this wide extension and a bandstand in the centre. You could sit on a deckchair and listen to the bands playing. We also saw bathing beauty contests, watched the children doing their "physical jerks", soldiers marching and the town crier show there too.

I cried the day the pavilion at the end of the pier burnt down. The fire raged for days despite the Pier Master and staff throwing buckets of sea water over it. The remnants of that lovely pavilion were washed ashore on the Stade. They think that the fire was started by a discarded cigarette. There had been a fire during one of the performances in the pavilion a few years before, but luckily it was quickly put out. This time the pier wasn't so lucky.

Reproduced with kind permission of the Hastings Pier & White Rock Trust.

Artist's impression of pier debris washing up on the Stade. Published in the Illustrated London News reproduced by kind permission of the Hastings Pier & White Rock Trust.

It could have been the end of the pier but after the war, they redesigned the pier, making it wider and giving it a new concert hall. Whilst not being as lovely as the original pavilion, it certainly had the shows. Dances and theatre – in fact I met my husband there, dancing. The pier also had more games, as well as the bowling alley, we played skee-ball and flash-o-ball regularly. I think we spent every Saturday on the pier!

The outdoor concerts were so popular you very often couldn't get a seat, so we would sit under the pier and listen to the music from there. Plus you could shelter from the rain under there too.

The Council extended the parade extension even more for more deckchairs. New viewing platforms were fitted onto the corners of the extension so you could stand, sheltered from the wind and gaze out to sea.

From time to time, we used to board the steamboat to go to Eastbourne, it was so much nicer than going on the train. We would take some sandwiches, and rugs to cover our legs, and see the pier get smaller and smaller until it disappeared as we approached Eastbourne.

When the Second World War started, refugees from France and Belgium arrived at the pier in Belgian tug boats. It was a sad sight seeing all these people fleeing for their lives.

The Pier was requisitioned by the RAF and Mr Torrance, the Acting Pier Master, was put on quarter pay. He was lucky though, so many of the other staff lost their jobs and some lost even their lives during the war. The centre of the Pier was breached and the whole thing filled with incendiaries so it could be blown up in the event of an enemy invasion.

Thankfully, this didn't happen and after the war, the pier reopened and some of the familiar faces, including Mr Torrance, returned. We continued seeing shows at the end of the Pier. Our grandchildren would also go to the Pier to see the new bands for the younger people. The Rolling Stones, The Who, Pink Floyd, Tom Jones and a strange fellow who played the guitar behind his back – Jimi Hendrix.

They took the bandstand down from the pier and put it in Warrior Square Gardens. We have been to a couple of concerts in the gardens. It was good to see the old bandstand again, but it was better on the pier. They built a moveable bandstand on the pier instead, which they wheeled around.

We all went to the Pier to see Princess Alice open the Hastings Embroidery in the Triodome. It was the 900th anniversary of the Battle of Hastings. The Triodome was a modern building built between the curved pavilion buildings.

About 20 years later, the pier was sold to a private company. The original owners, the Hastings Pier Company, had owned the pier since it was first established in the 1860s.

My grandchildren went to the pier to play on the amusements and in the playcentre which now lived in the Triodome. We went to play bingo. When my husband died, we decided to stand on the landing stage and sprinkled his ashes into the sea.

Sadly, shortly afterwards there was a terrible storm with 70 mile an hour winds which damaged the pier. The photos in the newspaper reminded me of seeing the remnants of the old pavilion on the Stade all those years ago. The boat landing stage was damaged and was never rebuilt. A few years later, some of my grandchildren went to the Pier to watch a boxing match which was being filmed. They were hoping to get on the television.

Work started again on changing the look of the pier. There were many complaints because the new owner of the pier made changes to the listed parts of the pier without planning permission. The company had to apply for retrospective permission but by then, the lovely 1930s façade had been removed.

Reproduced with kind permission of the Hastings Pier & White Rock Trust.

I have the sense that I have grown old with the Pier. She isn't the vivacious young girl she once was and neither am I, but we share many memories and she has been a source of delight for many.

Bibliography
Historic architectural drawings of the Parade Extension (dated 1916) Hastings Borough Council.
"Flying the Foam and some Fancy Diving" Directed by James Williamson, 1906 BFI Films
Images of the Pier kept at Hastings Museum and Art Gallery, Bohemia Road, Hastings
   "Steamer Aground" Hastings News 11th July 1873.
   "Pier Landing Stage" Hastings News 2nd May 1890.
   "Submarine Forest", Hastings News 21st July 1871
Records held at the East Sussex Records Office, Barbican House, High Street, Lewes.
"Hastings Pier Opens" Hastings News 9th August 1872.
Minutes from the Hastings Pier Company, 3rd November 1869 to 6 January 1872

The Lovers' Seat

The Lovers' Seat, once nestling high upon the cliffs at Fairlight, overlooked one of the finest views in all Sussex. The seat of stone, surrounded by rocks carved with countless initials of lovers, was a trysting place for lovers ever since it was first discovered. Sadly, it is no more.

Nevertheless, this delightful setting has left us with a story, a story of true love and a story to be told over and over again...

A Sailor's Tale

by Stanley John Arber

The gorse was a blaze of sunlight, beset in a mass of fern,
The path, a winding ribbon that rose with every turn,
The sky, a blue cupola reflecting the skylark's trill
When I met a Sussex sailor, whilst walking upon the hill.
"Are you looking for a seat, sir?" the sailor turned to ask,
And with his eyes a-twinkle, "you have indeed a task.
Across the glen, up yonder, that's where it used to be,
Till a raging storm and tempest sent it crashing to the sea."

"There's a yarn that local folk tell, though I'm sure I tell it right:
A tale about the Lovers' Seat that slipped away that night.
So sit you by the wayside, if time you have to dwell,
It's a tale of two young lovers, as I know it, I shall tell."
It was, in brief, the forenoon and my climb was void of shade,
So I chose to heed my informant and to rest as I was bade.
He leaned a little closer in a confidential way,
And his hand brushed back a forelock as I heard the stranger say,

"In the reign of George the Third, along this Sussex coast,
Where many a man was smuggling, as many a man would boast.
There sailed a Revenue cutter, The Stag, commanded by
A handsome young Lieutenant, Charles Lamb Esquire, of Rye.
He was born to a noble family, of excellent pedigree,
And was steadfast in his duty, and many friends had he.
He attended a Ball in Hawkhurst, in from the Sussex coast,
Where Samuel Boys of the Elfords, powerful and rich, was his host.

"At the Ball was Samuel's daughter, Elizabeth, sleek and young:
At once, as they danced in the moonlight,
                          the seeds of love were sprung.
And in time as their love grew stronger,
                          Charles did the honourable thing,
He sought her hand from her father, but refusal it did bring.
For Samuel's friends were powerful, eminent Lords and Kings,
And for his charming daughter he had cherished higher things.
But the flames of passion grew stronger, and the strain began to tell
And the lovers, ever defiant, quietly chose to rebel.

"Then Samuel Boys, unwisely, though succeeding in his quest,
Dispatched his lovelorn daughter to Fairlight Place, to rest
Unaware that the young lieutenant, who patrolled the Sussex shore,
Would accept this opportunity to rendezvous all the more
And Elizabeth, now befriended, saw too that she could meet
Her lover at the cliff top, alone at Lovers' Seat
A secret place for lovers, secluded by a ledge,
Bequeathed in time by nature, for lovers love to pledge.

"Alone, with deep emotion, though not bereft of hope,
They contrived a plan to marry, and a secret plan to elope.
Then discreetly, in a sunset, Charles steered his craft to land
Then climbed the path to Lover's Seat to take his lady's hand.
Down to the beach they hurried, to his boat on the evening tide
Then Charles set sail for Hastings with his love, and future bride,
Where a four-in-hand was waiting in the knell of evening light
Then they sped their way to London
                          through the darkness of the night.

"When the news was brought to the Elfords, Boys in a fit of rage
Rode fast his steed to London Town, not waiting for the stage.
Too late was he – the deed complete, it was as they had planned
Now married by the curate of St Clement Danes, The Strand.
Samuel Boys was ruthless, revengeful to the end.
He vowed to his errant daughter, his wealth she'd never spend
He cast her from the family home, then from his troubled mind
And died a very bitter man, his status much declined."

The sailor paused, entranced in thought, with eyes so blue and deep,
Then on his lips I sensed a smile; what secret did he keep?
He gazed towards the winding path that rose at every turn.
My silence held, I dared not speak lest I the sailor spurn.
"Retiring from the custom fleet," the sailor did resume,
"Charles drove his bride to Salehurst, where country pastures bloom
And dwelt in peace at Higham's House, but neither could foresee
That Charles would soon be restless, he would miss
                                    the bounding sea.

"Then came a day when, under sail, amid the Channel sound
Charles slipped and fell into the deep, was swept away and drowned.
He was given up on Bognor beach, upon the lonely shore
And rests in peace at Thakeham, *Charles Lamb – age – fifty four.*"
The sailor paused to take his breath, while from the harbour quay
I heard the sea birds calling across the sunlit sea.
My thoughts returned to his story, the sailor had told it well
Though I could see from his expression that more he had to tell.

18

"And Elizabeth?" I questioned softly, wondering what ere betide.
His blue eyes filled with sadness. "Ah yes," the sailor replied.
"Elizabeth, sweet Elizabeth." He paused, then to the cliffs looked he.
"Above Fairlight Glen, at Lovers' Seat, that's where she'll ever be."
I rose to thank my companion, the time was opportune
Not knowing that he'd departed, or that he had left so soon.
Then in the Cove at Fairlght, in the shelter of the Bay,
I saw the sails of a cutter fill, then quietly sail away.

Detail from the Millennium Chronicle of Hastings © 2000 Ron Nicola

The Fiddler on the Marsh

by Stanley John Arber

Across the marsh to Romney, beyond our shingled shore
I met a merry tinker, bound for Appledore.
He tarried by the wayside and on the stroke of noon
He raised his bow and fiddle a sweet and mellow fiddle,
    And played a simple tune.

No need had I to hurry, my day was free to spend,
The road lay bare before me, and not too far, the end.
I wondered why the tinker, who sat there on his dune
Would play his mellow fiddle, his sweet and mellow fiddle
    And never change the tune.

When out of view, I paused to rest beside a stream
To listen to his music, played as in a dream,
Borrowed from the angels, the notes came soft and low
While all the reeds were swaying, the reeds were gently swaying
    Swaying to and fro.

He did not play concertos or transcripts from Casals
Cadenzas, Obligatos or fast harmonic scales
Nor did he play Beethoven, Tchaikovsky or the rest
But on his mellow fiddle, his sweet and mellow fiddle,
    He played as he knew best.

I rose to take my leave, with tread so soft and light
And by the nestling church tower an inn came into sight
I slowed so I might listen, to hear the tinker play,
To hear his mellow fiddle, his sweet and mellow fiddle,
    To hear it fade away.

Then in my warm bedchamber there came a twilight glow
And through the open casement I felt a soft wind blow;
I saw the silver marsh road beneath the ghostly moon,
Is that the marsh winds calling, the soft winds gently calling
    Or the tinker's mellow tune?

Bluebell Wood

by Stanley John Arber

Once within a crowded wood
I heard a gentle sound
Arising from the forest floor
It echoed all around
Then softly o'er the dewy moss
My silent steps were bringing
The magic sound now close to me.
It was the bluebells ringing.

So merrily throughout the wood
The carillon did range
Then fairylike, a subtle switch
The bells rang out a change
And in the still of morning air
The bluebells gently swayed
Swung by strands of silken cord
From where the fairies played.

Then all around the forest floor
They rang from dawn till noon
And through the leaves a sunbeam fell
To twinkle to their tune
A spider strummed, a cricket danced
A silkworm came to see
While all the bells were ringing with
The humming of the bee.

So there I stood with bated breath
Lest I should break the spell
To see the tiny fairy elves
A dancing in the dell
And then a cry, a warning bell
It was then as I feared
At once the bluebells ceased to ring –
The fairies disappeared.

Detail from the Millennium Chronicle of Hastings © 2000 Ron Nicola

William's Picnic Spot

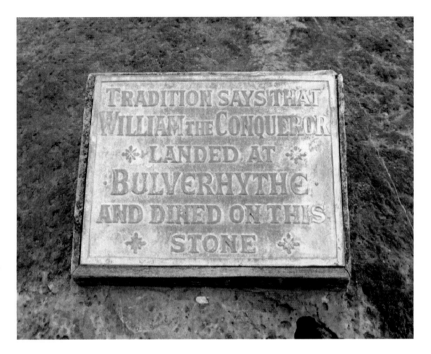

How do they know?

I'm sure the answer is in the history books somewhere but I'd rather leave it to the imagination. Ever since William the Conqueror appeared on the tourist posters after the war, inviting the people of Britain to invade Hastings once more, he has been an icon for local people. Stories and assumptions abound, so let us assume that an archaeologist, strolling along the shoreline at Bulverhythe, found traces of a garlic-sausage sandwich on this stone and so had it moved to St Leonards seafront to commemorate William's first meal in Hastings.

On the opposite page is William's panel from Ron Nicola's pictorial history of the town, 'The Millennium Chronicle of Hastings', a truly epic 'Vision of Hastings', created at the turn of the century to depict a thousand years of our history. The Millennium Chronicle is currently on display at St Clement's Church in the Old Town. *(KG August 2010)*

Tamarisk Town

by Christine A Hayward

An imaginary dialogue between Sheila Kaye-Smith (Sussex author, 1887-1956) and Christine Hayward (Secretary of the local Sheila Kaye-Smith Society and the Hastings & Rother Family History Society)

Sheila, you were counted amongst the leading English novelists of the early twentieth century and your books were sold worldwide. Nearly all your 31 novels were set in the Sussex and Kent countryside. Your first book, "The Tramping Methodist", was published in 1908 and your last book, "All the Books of My Life", was published posthumously in 1956.

You have been likened to the Regional Writers, Thomas Hardy and Mary Webb, but none of your books are now in print – although copies of some of them can still be found in second hand shops. The only one of your books to be filmed (in 1946) was "The Loves of Joanna Godden", in which Googie Withers, her husband John McCallum, and Jean Kent took the leading roles.

[It was the story of a woman farmer in a man's world on the Romney Marsh in the early 20th century and her determination to carry on farming after her father tragically died, combined with looking after her young sister.]

I hope you know that, thanks to the Sheila Kaye-Smith Society, there is now a blue plaque outside your childhood home in St Leonards.

Yes, and I am very flattered that such a thing should be thought of. I never expected I would still be remembered in 2009. I actually lived in Dane Road longer than I lived anywhere else in my life.

24

Of course, you were married in St Paul's Church in Church Road – just a few yards from where I live now, although the church is no longer there.

Oh yes, that was one of the best days of my life, you know, when I married my dear Penrose Fry. I never thought I would be married and I was 37 years old when I did so.

Hastings is 1066 country of course. It was only a few miles from here that William the Conqueror landed with his army and our town was one of the first to feel his heavy hand.

It certainly changed our world forever and Modern England probably started here. It would be interesting to go back and see how this country would have been if William had never come. I feel a part of the 1066 country; I missed Sussex so much when I married and went to live in London. After five years, we couldn't stay away any longer and moved to Northiam where I lived for the rest of my life.

As a native of Hastings – I was born here and have lived here all my life – which is quite a record – I would like to thank you for writing the book, "Tamarisk Town".

I called it Marlingate, and loosely based it on the Hastings I knew when I lived there. I was actually standing on the Tamarisk Steps, above Rock-a-Nore, when I had the idea to write the book.

You said in the book that the 'mass of Marlingate consisted of twists of streets and bristle of gables, its tumble of moss-grown roofs'. You called the two main streets by their original names: All Saints Street was Fish or Fisher Street and High Street was Market Street.

Yes, I wanted it to be as much like Hastings as possible – yet different.

You mentioned the Tamarisk Steps, between Rock-a-Nore and the old road under the East Hill, still called Tackleway, and you may remember that, from these steps, you can see a mulberry tree over the wall on the left. This is supposed to come from the original tree in Shakespeare's garden at Stratford-on-Avon. They say it was brought to Hastings by the famous 18th century actor, David Garrick, for his friend who lived here.

Yes, I remember that house and I've seen the tree.

The sea used to come up to the bottom of All Saints Street – Fish Street as you called it. The Bourne Stream, the only source of drinking water until the East Well was built in Rock-a-Nore, ran from the top of the street down to the Gut's Mouth, as it was inelegantly called for many years. It was here that my 4 x great uncle, Joseph Swain, aged 29, was killed by one of the sailors of the Coastguard Blockade Service, George England, on 13th March 1921 – not his lucky day!

Joseph was a fisherman and their boats were always searched when they came in from a night's fishing. He was also a smuggler and you can imagine that, when he came back in the morning, he would be tired and hungry and in no mood to be delayed once again. There was a fight between Joseph and George England as a result of which, George killed Joseph with one bullet from his pistol.

The Brasiers

George was actually charged with murder and tried for it but, although he was found guilty, he was allowed to resign from the Coast Blockade Service so long as he never returned to Hastings. Joseph left a widow, Mary, and six children – Joseph, Mary, Charlotte, Sarah, Sophia, Harriett and the youngest, Amelia, aged only ten months.

That is a very sad story and could have come from one of my books.

There were smugglers in my maternal grandmother's family too – the Brasiers.

If I had heard that story, I would perhaps have included it in my "Tamarisk Town".

At the top of All Saints Street, nearly opposite the church, was the Slough, later known as The Wilderness which you mentioned in "Tamarisk Town". My mother lived in the Old Town when she was a child and used to tell me how she and other local children played there. The land, then, was covered with bushes and blackberry brambles. Now it lies under The Stables Theatre car park, covered by a layer of concrete.

My mother and her family lived all over the Old Town, including Trafalgar Row and Woods Place – both of which you mentioned in your book – Mother and I once counted thirteen places where she remembered living but it certainly wasn't because they didn't pay the rent and were evicted, which happened to many of the poor families in the Old Town. Both my maternal grandparents were very hard working. Granddad worked at Breeds' Brewery for years.

I should like to have seen the town as it was then. I said in my book that 'The Slough was the source of the borough's water supply. Thrice a week (actually, it was every night at 5 oclock) the sluice-gates were opened and its waters overflowed into the Gut's Mouth Brook where the inhabitants of Marlingate, roused by the blast from a horn, could fill their household pots, pans and kettles – their water supply for the next 24 hours.

In my book, The Wilderness later became the town park. [Modelled on the real park in Hastings, Alexanda Park.]

On the other side of The Wilderness, on High Street (Market Street in your book), there still stands The Manor House, as it was known in those days, now a Home for Older People. It was originally in front of the Coney Banks where rabbits were encouraged so they could be used as meat for the table. John Collier, the great Town Clerk, lived there with his wife and many children in the 19th century and, after he died, his son-on-law Edward Milward, and his wife, Sarah, lived there.

I always thought it looked a nice, comfortable house and I used it for the home of my 'hero' Edward Moneypenny but I called it Gun Garden House. From his study window, Edward could see his territories sweep up almost to the crest of All Holland Hill (as I called the East Hill).

Further down High Street, just past Courthouse Street, stood The Maidenhead Inn which you named in your book the Maidenhood Inn, although you put it in a slightly different setting. Your

28

description seems to fit the Old Swan Hotel better. My mother worked at The Swan for a short time before she married my father. (The Old Swan Hotel was demolished in 1879 just before Sheila was born but a public house, also called The Swan was built in its place.)

And what about Harpischord House? Is that still there?

Yes, at the top of the Coburg Place steps, opposite St Clement's Church, stands the rather strangely shaped Harpsichord House, built into the cliff of the West Hill and stretching over the top of the path and steps which lead up to the Hill – altough you placed it over in Fish Street, Sheila.

Yes, I did. Well, it's been a pleasure to talk to you, Christine – and it has reallly brought all the ideas for my book back to me

Thank you, Sheila, for listening to me – and I will just mention that this little chat has made me decide to read "Tamarisk Town" again, for the first time since I was a teenager.

29

Death of The Swan

by D A Green

It was a sunny summer morning in Hastings, 1943. Jack, a sapper in the royal Engineers, was home on leave from the army on a 48-hour pass before being posted abroad. He was looking forward to a relaxing break and having a drink in his local pub before being hurled back into the madness of war.

"I'll just pop down to The Swan while you're getting the dinner," he told his wife, Clare.

"Good idea," she replied. "You'll be out of the way. I'll have a nice Yorkshire pudding waiting when you get back – with meat, gravy and roast potatoes."

He hesitated. She was nearly nine months pregnant. Their first baby was due at any time. "You're sure you'll be okay?" he asked.

"Course I will," she said. "I can come and get you if anything starts to happen."

He kissed her and left. They'd only been married for twelve months. They were young, and very much in love. This was hardly an ideal time to be bringing a baby into the world, what with a world war raging: rationing, food shortages and worst of all, constant air raids. Still, one day soon it must all come to an end and then their baby would have a better world to grow up in. Clare hoped it would be a boy who'd grow up to look like Jack and, maybe, if Britain won the war there wouldn't be any others so he wouldn't have to go and fight. Clare looked at the clock. She must get the cooking time right for that pudding. She wanted it to be perfect for Jack. It must rise beautifully, and be a crisp, golden brown.

She'd cry when his leave was over. He could easily get killed. But at least she'd got him for now – for two whole days. Suddenly, she felt a pain – so sharp that it took her breath away. She sat down in a chair to get her breath back. A little while later came another one. *Now, try not to panic*, she said to herself. *This must be it – the baby's coming!*

They were coming quite regularly now. She must hurry to The Swan to get Jack – and there they could phone for an ambulance. The timing was perfect. It was happening when he could be with her. She was so glad she wouldn't have to go through this ordeal all by herself and surely, because he would be there, nothing could go wrong. But there would be no Sunday dinner today!

Trying to keep calm, she turned off the oven, and hurried out into the street towards the pub. She saw a low-flying enemy bomber. It made a direct hit on The Swan. There was an almighty blast. The pub and nearby houses disintegrated into a mass of flames. Nobody could come out of that alive. She rushed towards the devastating scene, screaming with fear – and at the pains within her...

Sixty six years later two men stood in front of a small garden in the High Street in Hastings Old Town. They read a plaque attached to the small wire fence at the front. It said: *On this site stood the Swan Inn and 1, 2 and 3 Swan Terrace, destroyed by enemy action at about mid-day on Sunday 23 May 1943 with considerable loss of life.*

31

On this site stood
THE SWAN INN
& 1,2 & 3 SWAN TERRACE
destroyed by enemy action
at about mid-day on Sunday
23 May 1943 with considerable loss of life

The young man turned to the older one.

"So this is where it actually happened, Dad? It's what you've brought me from the other side of the world, from Australia, for."

"Yes, son. They rushed my mother to hospital and I was born about 11pm that same day. She named me Jack after my dead dad. I told you that one day I'd show you where your grandad died. After those two weeks in London, I wanted us to finish our holiday here. We'll have to tell our wives all about this when we get back. I'm glad this little memorial garden hasn't changed and they haven't built on it or anything since your mum and I came back ten years ago. It's just as I remember it – so quiet and peaceful. I took some photos of it to show your grandma before she died because, as you know, she never actually saw this place. She never came back to England again – not even for a holiday."

"How rotten to be born on the same day that your dad got killed," said the son.

"Of course, I never knew him but from what your grandma told me and all the photos I saw, he was an extraordinary bloke and I know he'd have been a great dad to me. She survived the war and did a good job, bravely carrying on and bringing me up alone. But after it ended she'd had enough of Britain: the austerity, the rationing and the cold, damp, grey weather, so we emigrated to Australia as '£10 poms'. She had it rough at first, living in a hostel, but she got a good

32

job, then a house, and things settled down. She made a new life for herself about as far away from England as she could get, but never re-married. I suppose she thought no other man could match up to her Jack."

They opened the small, iron gate and walked down the steps, through the garden and up some more steps. Sitting on a bench, they looked down on the scene. It was early June and the garden looked its very best, full of flowers, the scent of different coloured roses filling the air. At one side stood a notice board stating that the Swan Inn had been an old coaching inn, built in 1523, and that the life of the Swan came to an abrupt end during World War Two when, on May 23rd 1943 it was completely destroyed with much loss of life by a low-flying enemy fighter-bomber. It also stated that, ten years later, the site was acquired by the Corporation of Hastings to become a Memorial Garden to all those who died there in 1943. Across the narrow street, almost opposite the garden, was St Clement's church. Gazing across at the grey stone medieval building, the young man said, "Dad, it's as though that ancient church is looking down on this place and keeping a constant eye on it… Ironic that Grandad was a solider in that war but he died among civilians and not fighting the enemy.

"Yes son, it might seen strange to you but the last war was as much a civilian's war as it was a fighting servicemen's war. Towns and cities were bombed and millions of ordinary people killed. And that's how he died, enjoying a pint of beer alongside his friends and neighbours instead of in battle overseas. At least his didn't suffer."

"I'm glad I came," said the son. "I'll never forget this place."
As they turned to go, he looked back and said, "Goodnight, Grandad."

Riposo Health Hydro:

No, it was not a nudist colony!

by Richard Pitcairn-Knowles

Andrew Pitcairn-Knowles in about 1910

Almost exactly a century ago, on 23rd day of April 1910, Andrew Pitcairn-Knowles came from his home in Brussels to sign a twelve-week lease on 37 Cheriton Road, Folkestone at £3.3s.0d. per week. This was to be his base while he searched the south coast of England for a property suitable for conversion into a health hydro. From 1912 to 1962, a period of fifty years, this hydro was to help many patients but also to become a mystery for local people as strange rumours spread.

The fashionable seaside town of Hastings caught Andrew's imagination, and especially one of around fifteen large Victorian houses strung along The Ridge between Ore and Baldslow. The healthy air, 500 feet up, was a great attraction. Mssrs Beagleys, Estate Agents at 59 London Road, St Leonards presented him with "Ridgecroft," a substantial house with five large bedrooms, a stable block "with man's room over," standing in two acres, for £1,600. This house stood on The Ridge, near the top of Grange Road; only the stable block, Riposo Cottage, now remains, and Yew Tree Close occupies the site of the main house while the kitchen garden became Wrotham Close.

Ladies exercising on the lawn at Riposo in 1913

Andrew had spent the first forty years of his life on the Continent. Born in Rotterdam in 1871, registered as British, he was the son of a wealthy Scottish wool merchant, William Pitcairn-Knowles (1820-1894) and a Polish opera singer. His parents retired to Wiesbaden, his father aged about fifty-five, and Andrew was educated there.

William Pitcairn-Knowles was well known as a collector of Old Master drawings and when these were sold, following his death, Andrew and his brother James each used their considerable inheritance in markedly different ways.

James, an artist, married a wealthy illegitimate daughter of Napoleon III and they built a castle, Freudenberg, (still standing) near Wiesbaden, but they parted after less than ten years and lost most of their wealth.

Andrew first studied chemistry and photography and then, aged about twenty-one, settled in Berlin to indulge his passion for sport, launching the illustrated sporting magazine, *Sport im Bild*, in 1893. In 1899 he married a Scottish girl, Margaret Gardner. Their son, Gordon, was born in 1900.

Andrew persuaded his wife and son to travel with him throughout Europe while he wrote articles, illustrated with his own photographs, on subjects as diverse as lobster farming, kite flying,

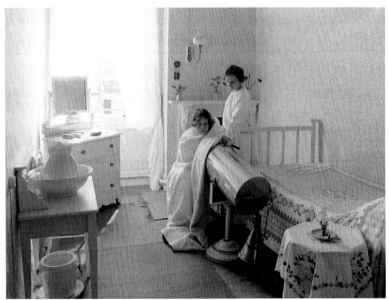

Steam bath in Room 5 at Riposo

Sun bathing enclosure

horse racing and cock fighting. They moved home to Paris and then Brussels. It was while they were on a visit to Corsica writing about bandits and goatherds that his son was badly injured by a kick in the abdomen from a mule, and the family had to rush back by carriage, boat and several trains to Berlin, where Andrew knew he would find excellent medical help. Having experienced the Natural Therapeutic methods used to cure his son, Andrew then decided that these ideas should be brought to England.

The saying that behind every successful man there is a woman is often true. Margaret was to become a mainstay of Riposo Health Hydro, as the establishment was to become known. An extract from a long and touching letter from Margaret, while with her sister in Jersey, to Andrew in Brussels, dated 16th September 1911, illustrates her support:

My own darling Hubby

I was so awfully, awfully glad to get your sweet letter this morning, as I have been feeling anything but happy the last 3 days in spite of the nice time they are giving us here. I had just sent off a p.c. telling you the train when I got your letter.

I had so often feared lately that we would make a muddle of our lives, and I <u>know</u> that it is my lack of sympathy and understanding which causes it, but surely when we know how much we love each other we can manage not to do so, but on the contrary, to lead more useful and better lives. ... ...

If I could only understand your ideas better, I am sure we would find ourselves truly happy, but I always feel I am a drag on you as I am a very ordinary minded and too practical kind of woman. I know I have become much more so than I was, instead of less, why I don't know unless it has been the life we have led that has made me so.

All the same I am convinced that the "Nature Cure" place is just the very work that you need, and of course you can depend on me putting all my heart and soul into the work with you. The only thing is that I feel I am/may not satisfy you.

I have <u>no objection at all</u> to us starting the place – <u>on the contrary</u> – but I am often afraid you will get the blues in England as you always find life there so narrow.

I don't think Gordon should put you off your scheme as you are a young man still and he has still 10 years to live before he is a

"man", and by that time he may have become a very convinced
"Vegetarian" from the humanitarian point of view as well as from
the health point of view. ... ...
     Au revoir, till tomorrow evening shortly after 7 I hope.
                   Your own Wifey"

Negotiations for Ridgecroft became drawn out. Several more visits to Hastings had to be made, and completion finally took place in 1911. Andrew left the remainder of his money invested in Germany through both wars with disastrous effect on the family fortunes. He continued to buy parcels of land to a total of ten acres, however five of these acres, abutting Hillside Road, remained as fields and are now covered by the houses of Chanctonbury Drive, Ranmore Close and Newlands Close.

    The house was to be converted and planning applications for wooden chalets to be erected in the grounds were made – eventually at least thirty were constructed.

Two of more than thirty Riposo chalets

But first some cleaning of the house was offered when Alfred Meadows Elliott, Solicitor of 6 Cambridge Road forwarded a letter on 10th January 1912 from *"Mrs Major the person who looks after "Ridgecroft" at the present time."*

38

The letter, showing such pride in her work, is quoted in full:

7, Landview
St Helens
Hastings

Mr Elliott.
Dear Sir,

In reply to your letter I shall be very pleased to do down "Ridgecroft". Of course I shall not be able to do it down in 2 days as it is such a state as you know. The grates will take a day if they want them cleaned and of course there is no water it is turned off at the main and I cannot do anything without water and I think before the water is turned on a plumber ought to see the pipes to see there is no leakages I know everything was alright when Mrs Russell left but but that is over a year ago now and the tanks ought to be all cleaned out as they have got in rather a bad state. Of course I will see after all this if you like. Of course I thoroughly understand everything as I have worked in Ridgecroft for over 20 years. I will find coals soap, and soda and black lead for grates and everything and scrub it down for £1:0:0 of course I will wash venetian blinds and clean windows inside also paint. If you will kindly let me know I will start at once.

Yours very sincerely
M. A. Major

Advertisements were placed in periodicals of the time, both in England and Andrew's beloved Germany, and Riposo took in its first visitors later in 1912. At Easter 1913, unable to leave his German sporting life behind, Andrew invited a representative German hockey team to train at Riposo, and arranged for them to stay at The Queens Hotel with a full programme of entertainment and hockey matches against Deal, Folkestone, and Philistines (Richmond) and the home team, South Saxons. The Council supported the event and the German flag hung above the Town Hall. The team was entertained at the Grange School and then at Riposo as the report on the tour in *"Lawn-Tennis und Golf"* states:

... The beautiful surroundings with the view down to Hastings & St Leonards and to the glittering Channel made a deep impression ... This area is called 'one of the beauty spots of the South of England' ... We returned to the Knowles's for a performance by the Boy Scouts by torchlight, attended by a large number of invited guests. The performance closed with a rendition of "Wacht am Rhein" ... the scouts had taken the trouble to learn the song in German, which deserves a special mention.

Andrew must have been heartbroken when Germany and Britain were at war just over a year later. Throughout the 20s and 30s Riposo boomed. Activities included lectures, outings, picnics, paper chases, cookery demonstrations and lantern slide shows. Before antibiotics were discovered, before modern anaesthesia and surgery, the regimes at Riposo helped many with arthritic complaints, skin problems, digestive disorders and weight problems. Vegetarianism was important and various quite heroic diet regimes were applied as well as massage and, of course, many forms of hydrotherapy and exercise. When not on one of the strict diets food was always in the Mediterranean style – vegetarian salads, fruit, some eggs and cheese and occasional fish. At last, a century later, the consensus is that a Mediterranean diet is the healthiest. Gold, silver and two bronze medals for vegetarian meals were won by Riposo at The Universal Cookery & Food Exhibition at Earls Court in 1930. Emphasis was also placed on fresh air, dew walking and sun bathing – the last being always discreetly in the nude with ladies and gentlemen's enclosures separate and a special family enclosure. This is why Riposo had its rumoured reputation as a nudist camp!

The chalets were double skinned, originally heated by gas fires and lit by gas mantles. Maids carried hot water, meals on trays and changes of bedding to the chalets in all weathers – and some of the chalets were two or three hundred yards from the main house. It was a good life, at a slow pace, for all concerned but in the third millennium patients would expect more creature comforts and staff would refuse such conditions of work!

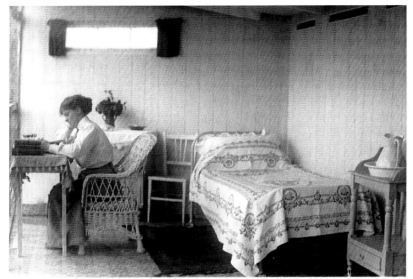

Interior of a chalet at Riposo

Badminton court at Riposo

By 1939, Britain was at war again. Hastings – and Riposo – were much more vulnerable this time. 'Tip and run raids' were a frequent experience as planes raced low over Romney Marsh, avoiding

41

RADAR, and skimmed over the chimney pots on The Ridge to drop their bombs on Hastings on their way out to sea. Of course no patients were around at this time – travel to the south coast was banned much of the time. V1 Doodlebugs were a menace towards the end; shrapnel from anti-aircraft guns damaged the chalet roofs and every front window of the main house was blown out by a doodlebug exploding in the woods nearby.

Recovery at Riposo after the damage of WW2 was slow but steady, and many patients passed through Riposo in the 1950s until, first Andrew died, aged 84, in 1956 (his wife lived on another ten years), and then his son, Gordon, died in 1963. After fifty successful years it was time for Riposo to close.

~~~

Robertson Street 1920s photo from the collection at Hastings Reference Library, East Sussex Library Service

Who Am I?*

by Donald E Valentine

I came to live here by the sea –
at the time, another evacuee.
I was billeted out at Silverhill,
a little east of Draper's smock-mill.

My livery was green and white
and must have looked a pretty sight.
Inside and out were perfectly cleaned.
Was this the day of which I'd dreamed?

Out of the gates, turn left at The Clarence
and stop by the store which had all the garments:
socks, shoes, shirts, coats, ties, perhaps
everyone knew you could find it at Apps.

This day I ran on the No 2 route
(or circular route if you want to be cute)
forward and left into Bohemia land
to see churches, Post Offices, shops, hand in hand.

By St Paul's Road was a post which rendered
t'was just a mile to Hastings town centre.
A terrace of elegant houses seen on the right
while Summerfields School was hidden from sight.

Magdalen Road was the stop for the Catholics
Attending St Thomas's with its tall candlesticks.
Alight next stop for John's Place Museum
where visitors and locals found plenty to teach em.

The Oval, and views of the pier were seen,
White Rock Gardens with its bowling greens
and the clock, annually given a new look
with miniature plants – and a theme, to book.

---

* Answer at end

It was never 'the RESH', just 'the hospital'
with outpatients and wards behind a high wall
and Cambridge Road had a church for the Methodists
while the Post Office boasted a floor for telephonists.

Opposite, the façade of the church Congregational
and Tabernacle adjacent – very interdenominational.
There was nothing like the Memorial clock tower
to look at and hear quarterly chimes every hour.

Never forgot the majestic Ritz:
visits treasured for its organ and flicks
or maybe instead, the Gaiety or Plaza
where newsreels were included not a penny extra.

Woolworths, Sainsburys, Macfish and Demarco
also Samuels, Mozley, Maynards, Lyons & Co.
Wellington Square had offices of Authority,
guest houses and Practices (anatomically).

Departmental Mastins and Cinema de Luxe –
before it became a bingo hall – matter of luck.
St Mary in Castle, famed for its well
Pelham Arcade's shops, with goodies to sell.

Little boats and lifeboat opposite The Cutter
"Nethouses ahead!" called out my conductor.
Children in boats trying hard not to knock,
finished the day with candyfloss and rock.

Driving in High Street – a navigational skill –
two-way traffic, which rarely stood still.
Trolleys, buses, Maidstone and East Kent.
Timetables were honoured, however we went.

Air raid shelter built on Torfield land
for use by Old Town folk, I understand.
Bombs fell in the years I was there
but thankfully I wasn't damaged anywhere.

Climbing the hill to the village called Ore
with its cinema, theatre and House for the Poor,
Hare, Hounds and Oddfellows, Home & Colonial,
all most friendly and very sociable.

The Ridge was the original London road
from Hastings past Frewen's abode
Coghurst was beyond the Gatehouse Lodge – a sight
as we wound our way to the Hastings height.

The next mile or so could be called 'the school run'.
Learning establishments passed one by one:
Bright girls debussed at the school called the High,
Then St Margaret's, Hurst Court and Hydneye.

The cemetery was the St Helen's terminus
for other routes of the trolleybus
but my route continued, on past the church
and schools, and trees of oak and birch.

How I enjoyed Route No 2 – the part which was rural,
with Hydro and farms – and smells so agricultural!
A tin church heralded the hamlet of Baldslow
but for how long would town planners allow it so?

The Harrow was an old coaching inn
and for me a place to check in.
From here I did not need a shove
just ensure my shoes stayed on the wires above.

Downhill now, speed had to be resisted
to be ready to stop whenever requested
more schools to pass, where pupils were triers
and head for the next stop, known as The Briers.

Little shops at Silverhill – would they remain?
After I'd gone, what would be the same?
Thank you, Hastings, forever by the sea,
for all the joy that serving you gave me.

By 2010 I will have been gone
some 51 years since trundling along.
I was just 20 years old when taken away
to rest in peace, some wise men would say.

'Clean up Hastings' is still the cry
but how much cleaner it was when I
carried you in my diesel-free bus
in which there seemed room for all of us!

At the junction of Grange Road on the last day of operation.
Photo taken by the late Lyndon Rowe.

*Who am I? The Sunbeam Trolleybus of course (working out of
Silverhill depot until May 1959)

On Hastings

by Kathleen Upton

I moved to Hastings when I was seven years old, my father had just left the navy after many years in service and had secured a job at Hastings Post Office so we left our house in Chatham and came back to the area where he had been born. I went with my sister, who is a year older than me, to St Paul's School. We always boasted it was the best school in town, a strict but fair school with excellent teachers and one of the highest scholarship results in town.

St Paul's School, photo from the collection at Hastings Reference Library, East Sussex Library Service

We lived in a flat near Silverhill, with its row of shops, two doctors' surgeries, three churches and Alexandra Park nearby. All these years later it hasn't changed very much and still has that 'village' feeling. Hastings town itself has seen many changes and, I suppose to compete with other towns, has produced a shopping precinct, car parks and all the other features which are mirrored in almost every town. In those pre-war years, we seemed to have everything any town could want. In the centre was the Albert Memorial, built to commemorate the death of Queen Victoria's beloved Albert. The clock was always a focal point and around the actual memorial, the flowerbeds were immaculate as were the beds all along the sea front.

47

Our parks were beautifully kept and coach loads of visitors came for the day and would picnic there. The bandstand was often in use. Military bands would visit in the summer and on Sundays crowds of people would be there. A man called Uncle Joe would conduct community singing for us all to join in. Apart from lovely Alexandra Park, we had other gardens. The White Rock with well kept bowling greens, still in use today; Gensing Gardens, off London Road, smaller but with a nice play area, swings and other delights including a small boating pond; St Leonards Gardens off Maze Hill and Warrior Square, where in spring the tulips were a brilliant sight.

Pre-war Hastings had some large and well run stores: Mastins was a family-run concern selling materials, hats, ready made dresses and suits and all kinds of accessories. Their staff could live in. There were rooms above the shop for girls from villages who couldn't get back to their homes in the evenings, as often shops stayed open till 9pm and later on Saturdays. Another similar shop was Willshins in Queens Road. Mr Willshin was at one time the Mayor of Hastings. Plummer Roddis (now Debenhams) was the largest store in town and still occupies the same site. White and Norton (now a charity furniture store) was rather an expensive store, priced beyond most 'working class' families. Philpots at the St Leonards end of the promenade was probably the most exclusive of all and included genuine fur coats in their range of goods.

Hastings boasted a number of cinemas. The Ritz stood where ESK is now; The Plaza, later the Orion, was where Yates' Wine Bar stands; The Gaiety, now the Odeon, is the one original cinema still operating; The De Luxe is now a bingo hall; the Regal is now Ocean House (the Income Tax Office); the Curzon in Norman Road now houses a builders' merchants, and a very nice cinema in Warrior Square was called the Elite. During the war it suffered a direct hit and was completely destroyed. It was finally rebuilt and a grand opening planned. The film was to be "The Great Fire of London" (or similar title). Sadly, just as it was to be opened it caught fire and was completely destroyed again. No-one ever knew what caused the fire but it never reopened and a block of flats now occupies the site. The final one was the Silverhill Picture House, later renamed the Roxy. For fourpence on a Saturday morning you could go and watch a main picture, a second film – usually a cowboy one, and a newsreel. The family that ran the cinema were called the Meatyards. One of the Miss Meatyards was formidable, no-one dared misbehave if she was on duty. She would appear silently, lift the luckless perpetrator by the ear and march them out of the cinema. They would be banned from the next performance, so most of us would be on our best behaviour.

The White Rock Pavilion, now called Theatre, had plays and shows practically all the year. The Court Players, a local drama group, were, I believe, originally on the pier but when the war started the pier was closed, so they moved to the White Rock.

They performed a different play each week. What wonderful memories they must have had, always acting one play, rehearsing another and learning their parts for yet another. A friend and I, who worked together, had a half day on Wednesdays (when all shops shut) and we always went to the Court Players. I believe we only paid ninepence and we always sat in the front of the upstairs balcony. I still remember some of the names: Martin Caroll and his wife Sylvia played the leads, assisted by Keith Lorraine and Elsie Henigan who always played the naughty parts. There were several other regular actors whose names I can't remember. Even during the frequent hit-and-run raids in wartime the 'show went on'. Nobody wanted to go to the air raid shelters underneath the theatre, and ruin the play.

Each August we had Carnival Week, now replaced by Old town Week. Starting with school holidays in August, a group of local young people formed a club. I think they called themselves the 'Revellers'. They wore fancy dress costumes and caused mayhem all week, playing pranks on unsuspecting folk – all very good humoured and jolly.

£1,000 Bathing Belle Contest.

See the pick of Britain's Beauties in a contest Nationally organised
by
THE DAILY SKETCH
at the

Aerial Displays	Biggest & Brightest	Tennis Drives

Aerial Displays
High-speed Acrobatics
and Flour-bag Bombing.

★

DAGENHAM
    GIRL PIPERS

★

TINY TOTS PARADE

AQUATIC
CARNIVAL
in
EUROPE'S
FINEST
BATHING
POOL.

ROLLER SKATING
DISPLAYS
Hockey & Rugby on Skates.
Torchlight Display.

Biggest & Brightest Carnival ever held on the South Coast

Note the Dates—

SEPT. 7ᵗʰ to 14ᵗʰ

7 Gorgeous Days . .
Glamorous Nights
of Gaiety.

GLITTERING
PROCESSIONS
DAY and NIGHT

TWO GREAT
BATTLES *of* **CONFETTI**

GIGANTIC
FAIR AND CIRCUS
Bigger and Better than Last Year.

Tennis Drives
Competitions Daily.

★

TREASURE HUNTS

★

STADIUM VARIETY
AND RODEO SPORTS

★

CHILDREN'S
FANCY DRESS
PARADES

CARNIVAL
QUEEN
CROWNED
by a
FAMOUS
FILM
STAR.

WINKLE CLUB
DANCES
on the Famous Island.

GREAT CARNIVAL BALL.
Dancing all the Week. ❖ ❖ Open Air Dancing.

Join the King of the Rebellers and His Court of Merrymakers! ●
    ● *Come in Fancy Dress and stay in Fancy Dress the whole Week.*

THE HASTINGS PRINTING CO., PORTLAND PLACE & TOWER ROAD.

1935 Carnival poster from the collection at Hastings Reference Library, East Sussex Library
Service

51

A big fair would be held on the Oval: swing boats, roundabouts, chair-o-planes and the big attraction – the Wall of Death. An enormous drum-shaped structure with motorbikes roaring around, doing criss-cross manoeuvres with each other. And the spectators standing around the upper rim, holding our breath as the bikes roared up to the very top. One year, and I cannot remember it happening again, I saw two miserable-looking lions in cages outside. I realise now that they must have been sedated because they were strapped to the back of the motorbikes and took part in the performance. Performing animals were common pre-war. Thank goodness that would not be allowed now.

Our two piers were also popular. St Leonards pier had a car racing rink, roller skating area, shops and an ice cream parlour where for one penny you could buy the biggest cornet in town. Sadly, during the war the middle of the pier was blown up to prevent any enemy landings. Afterwards, a fire destroyed what was left so the remains were removed, leaving only Hastings pier in place. Now, even that pier may be doomed, the metal structure needs complete renewal and the cost will be prohibitive. We live in hopes that a reputable buyer will be found.

We had a tent on the beach next to Hastings Pier. A licence had to be obtained and I believe it was 12 shillings a year for the right to tie your tent to an enormous iron ring in the wall in the hope that it wouldn't be washed away during one to the summer storms. I know we lost at least one tent in this way. My sister and I would often go straight to the beach after school with our swimsuits so that we could get into the sea as quickly as possible. Our mother would come down about five o'clock, bringing drinks and sandwiches. It was like a large social club as we knew all the families in their tents and many friendships were made, lasting in my case up to the present day.

Another attraction on the beach was Biddy the Tubman. He was a fisherman from the Old Town and he would paddle along from there to the Warrior Square area. Any children who wanted to go in his tub could go for a quick ride and then he would suddenly spin the tub, faster and faster, and tip it up so we fell out and had to swim back to 'our beach'. What fun! People would throw coins which he donated to local charities. There was never another character like Biddy.

Biddy the Tubman: Detail from the
Millennium Chronicle of Hastings © 2000 Ron Nicola

The White Rock Baths were of Olympic standard. That was where most of us learned to swim. My sister and I belonged to the

'Ducklings' and were taught by a fierce lady who always wore a rubber apron and Wellington boots. We were terrified of her. She paraded up and down the baths carrying a long pole with a hook at the end, supposedly to fish out a child in trouble but mainly used for prodding people between the shoulders for not swimming fast enough. The diving boards seemed enormously high and standing on the top one and hearing her shout, *NOW!* ... she haunted my dreams.

At the far end of St Leonards were some small but beautiful gardens and a bowling green and then – the pride and joy of the town, the Bathing Pool. Terraced all round for spectators as well as swimmers it was, we were told, built to Olympic standards. After the war, it never re-opened for the general public but became a kind of holiday camp with chalets for holidaymakers. It gradually fell into disuse, the chalets were demolished, the pool drained and closed. Now the area is overgrown with grass and there never seems to be a useful purpose for it. The enormous diving board where divers from all over the country would come to compete, the galas and in autumn, the firework displays – all gone. What a loss to the town.

Photo from the collection at Hastings Reference Library, East Sussex Library Service

Then came that unforgettable day, not long before my thirteenth birthday, when in church on that Sunday morning, the minister announced from the pulpit ... *that no such agreement has been reached and England is now at war with Germany* ... our lives, and Hastings, were changed for ever.

Detail from the Millennium Chronicle of Hastings © 2000 Ron Nicola

Childhood Holiday

by Joe Fearn

It was the day
that saw Sisyphus
detach his hands
from the boulder,

straighten up
his back with an
awkward twist,

and run from the mountain,
his eyes sharp as diamonds,
fixed on bright, untamed horizons.

The sun, the sea, the sand, the pier,
the cockles and mussels, candyfloss and beer.
The donkey rides at two-an'-a-kick,
the cheeky girls; kiss me quick.
The Mods, the Rockers, the Teddy Boys,
Suede Heads, Greasers, Diddi-coys,
those one-armed bandit places
that paid me out in jacks and aces;

Oh Hastings!
I thought I'd found the lost Atlantis
on the Sussex coast,
your green unguarded gold
within my reach.

56

A Hot Day in Hastings

by Joe Fearn

At St Leonards-on-Sea
in the heat haze,
Marine court is sailing
down the road to Hastings.

Shaven headed men walk past,
Strange how Hastings men disguise their baldness
by becoming even balder.
Children are enjoying the traditional sights;
Pelham Island, the Funicular Railway, the Smugglers' Caves,
the black wooden fishing huts on the Stade,
expensive parked cars plastered in seagull poo.

On discovering the English Channel,
one child dressed like a Spice Girl
comments, "It's a pile of water."

It's pirate week,
bunting is stretched between shops;
seven seagulls on a high wire
form the first bars of a sea-shanty
down George Street.

Saucy-postcard ladies adorn the seafront,
an old man is on the sea-view bench
fast asleep,
his head on his chest,
his crumpled face like someone screwed it up and threw it
at the nearby waste bin and missed.

I think of my mother,
smiling in her wheelchair, as frail as moonlight in daytime,
and how she would have liked
this hot day in Hastings.

Photo of Mr and Mrs Daft

by Joe Fearn

The sky here
isn't actually blue,
it only appears blue
because it reflects the sea,

which itself isn't really blue,
it just reflects the sky.

It sounds daft, but somehow works,

like the marriage of Mr and Mrs Daft,
shown here in Hastings in 1915.

Mr Daft is stunning in khaki,
Mrs Daft is peaches and cream.

She will run a shop in St Leonards,
he will board a troopship
and be blown to pieces
in the Dardanelles.

What Hastings Means To Me

by Kevin Boorman

Quite simply, Hastings is my favourite place, and the most important place in the world to me. I am very proud of the fact that I was born and brought up in the Old Town of Hastings, and have lived there ever since, despite working outside the town for over twenty years, much of that time spent commuting to and from London.

I'm also pleased that all five of my children went to Dudley Infants School, my old school, and also the school that my mum went to! I chaired the governing body there for a number of years, indeed I was a parent governor for nearly twenty years, yet can still remember my very first days there back in the early 1960s, tearfully waving goodbye to Mum as I watched her disappear over the brow of the hill in Harold Road.

I am also very proud of the fact that I come from an Old Town family. We have traced our ancestors back for over 200 years; one was reputedly hanged for smuggling in the early 19th Century. But my relations have redeemed themselves since, as my great granddad was second cox of the lifeboat for many years. My nan was named after a boat the Hastings lifeboat rescued after a particularly difficult launch in 1908, which featured on a series of Judges postcards: my great grandmother was over six months pregnant with my nan at the time, and hadn't expected to see her husband again, so dangerous was the sea. When the lifeboat returned safely, my nan was given the middle name of Amy, after the barge the lifeboat rescued.

And my nan's brother, 'Uncle George' as I used to call him (George Moon), was cox of the Hastings Lifeboat at the time of the Dunkirk evacuation, and took our lifeboat to Dover. He was then relieved by a Royal Navy crew, and was very bitter that he wasn't able to take the lifeboat across the channel. Later, in the early sixties, I used to love visiting 'Uncle George' in the old lifeboat house, where he used to work. I liked to think I was helping him, but looking back I'm sure I was more of a hindrance than a help but he still didn't seem to mind me going.

I've been a huge fan of the lifeboat ever since and, right up until the maroons were replaced by pagers, I've always raced to watch the lifeboat launch whenever I heard the two loud bangs. Often the sea was calm, but I've seen some atrocious launches in Force 9 and 10 seas, too, and have had the utmost respect for the brave lifeboatmen (and now lifeboatwomen) ever since. Most of these were, and still are, volunteers, of course.

I've always loved watching the fishing boats too, both as a child and more recently. When I was commuting, the early morning starts weren't as bad, and the prospects of a day in London less daunting, if I could see the fishing boats plodding out to sea soon after 5am when I walked to the station to catch an early train.

I remember missing the Old Town, the sea, and 'the glen' (Ecclesbourne Glen) when I was at university in London. I deliberately chose weekday-only digs so that I had to come home every weekend, and most Sundays I would walk around the twittens of the Old Town just enjoying the unique atmosphere, always pausing at the lookout, at the bottom of Tackleway, to enjoy the views over the fishing beach to the harbour. But even that wasn't always enough. I often used to come home on a Wednesday afternoon, which was free time, just to enjoy walking our dog over the glen! Then I'd go back to London…

Old Towners have always been rebellious – some say nothing has changed – and I remember how angry we all were back in the late

1960s when we were told that for safety reasons (who says health and safety is a recent phenomenon?!) the carnival couldn't come to the Old Town. It always used to start at the Bathing Pool, come along the seafront to the Old Town, then go back along the seafront to the Memorial and up Queens Road to finish in the park. But then we were told it couldn't come to the Old Town…so what did we do? We organized our own Old Town Carnival, which I'm pleased to say still continues to this day. And, like most Old Towners, it seemed, I took part in that first Old Town Carnival – perched on the back of a builders' lorry driven by my granddad.

One of the things that surprises me most is how much Hastings has changed. Most people's perception is that Hastings hit a low point in the 1990s, but I actually think it was probably in the 1980s when we were at our lowest ebb. I think the turning point was the building of Priory Meadow, although I didn't think so at the time, as I've still got fantastic childhood memories of watching Sussex play there – usually against Kent. As a schoolboy I was very excited to get the autographs of Tony Greig and John Snow from Sussex, and Alan Knott of Kent – real names from the past now!

It's just not cricket... soon to be a multi-million pound shopping centre

This is the scene of demolition at the old cricket ground site. By 1997 it will be home to more than 50 shops Exclusive picture:Derek Casper

Cutting from Hastings and St Leonards Observer, archive held at Hastings reference library, inset: The statue of the cricketer that now stands in the shopping centre square.

But Hastings really did have its problems even then, as the growth of cheap continental holidays marked the end of Hastings as a traditional family seaside resort. The hotels became more and more shabby, eventually becoming hostels and care homes.

It is interesting, too, how different parts of the town have changed. My dad was born in Union Street, in what is now known as Central St Leonards, and my mum lived in the Croft, in the Old Town. At the time, my dad was moaned at by his mum for going out with someone below his station, because she came from the Old Town! Now, of course, the Old Town is one of the most sought after areas of Hastings, while Central St Leonards is one of the most deprived.

I was fortunate enough to go to Hastings Grammar School as it then was (William Parker now, of course), but really had the micky taken out of me because I was from the Old Town, and had the distinctive Old Town accent (which some say I still retain to this day. If so, I'm proud of that, too!).

Interestingly, of the hundred or so boys in my year at the Grammar School, hardly any still live in Hastings; I think that's really sad. Equally sad is that even now a lot of young Hastingers choose not to stay here, but are attracted to the bright lights of London and elsewhere. (Hastingers come from Hastings, Hastonians went to the Grammar School, so I'm actually both a Hastinger and a Hastonian!)

But as I said before, I have no doubt at all that things have changed for the better. Back in the 1970s, the main attractions were the pier, the bathing pool, St Clements Caves, the Castle and the lifts (I used to love watching the water pour out from the tanks of the East Hill Lift car when it arrived at the bottom, and am really pleased that East Hill Lift has recently reopened, with its new wooden coaches resembling those of my childhood, so much better than the fibreglass replacements which ran from the mid 1970s until just a few years ago).

Apart from the East Hill Lift, the only real attraction in Rock-a-Nore Road was the Fishermen's Museum which, although lovely (and, truthfully, little changed since then) hardly ever seemed to open. My memory tells me that it only opened on summer Sunday afternoons. I'm sure in reality it was more frequent than that, but it really wasn't open very often. Indeed, the rest of Rock-a-Nore Road included a derelict drill hall, and an old factory, equally unattractive, and a far cry from the Shipwreck & Coastal Heritage Centre and Aquarium we see there today. As I mentioned above, right up until the 1970s the Old Town was not the heaving, seething visitor destination it is today, but simply home to the fishermen and their families.

Now, of course, we've got some fantastic new visitor attractions, and some superb refurbished ones. Smugglers Adventure is so much better than the old St Clement's Caves I remember as a child, with a grumpy guide taking us around. (Even if there is no evidence that the caves were really ever used by smugglers.) In fact The Caves is probably my single favourite attraction in Hastings, simply because it is so unique. And I also enjoy telling people that my mum lived in a cave – she slept and was schooled in St Clement's Caves in the Second World War, of course!

And the Adventure Golf on the seafront is fantastic, hugely popular with visitors, and attracting a lot more people than the old sandpit and donkey rides that used to occupy that site when I was young.

Visitor accommodation has also improved considerably. What we might lack in quantity, following the widespread closure of hotels in the 1970s, we more than make up in quality, with three five star gold bed & breakfasts, one each in St Leonards, the town centre, and the Old Town (Hastings House, Black Rock, and Swan House respectively). That really does put Hastings at the centre of the growth in quality niche visitor accommodation.

And Hastings hasn't just improved from a visitor perspective. Too often we focus on the negative aspects of the town, yet step off a train at the new railway station and you cannot miss the Sussex Coast College Hastings building, nor the University Centre Hastings as you walk down Havelock Road. Just opposite, in Lacuna Place and Priory Square we've got two state of the art office buildings, and more jobs being created by the business park under construction on Queensway.

Most importantly, the community spirit of Hastings lives on. The creation of the Old Town Carnival over forty years ago was just the start of community events, long before they were labelled as such. We now have Jack In The Green and Bonfire, both absolutely fantastic pedestrian processions, as well as Old Town Week, which has also been going for over fifty years. Although nominally a visitor attraction, most of the events really are just an excuse for the Old Town to let its hair down.

I'm also really pleased that Hastings Day, indeed Hastings Week, continues. I can still remember my very first glimpse of the Queen, back in October 1966; I was at All Saints School then, and remember passing my brother (who was still at Dudley) excitedly waiting for her to appear. We got a very brief wave as she sped down Old London Road, on her way to open the triodome on the pier. Hastings Day, and Hastings Week, grew from the excitement of that celebration of the 900th anniversary of the Battle of Hastings.

Detail from the Millennium Chronicle of Hastings © 2000 Ron Nicola

So to conclude, I know Hastings isn't perfect, goodness me I've lived here long enough to know that. But nor does it deserve the poor media coverage it received, which I think was at its worst in the late 1990s, when we were 'Costa Del Dole' and 'Hellhole-On-Sea.' What absolute rubbish! Hastings is definitely not your bland south coast resort. It's got an edginess, a bohemian air, but that makes it a great place to live and work, as well as visit. I really wouldn't want to live anywhere else.

64

Enough Edge

by Peter Saunders

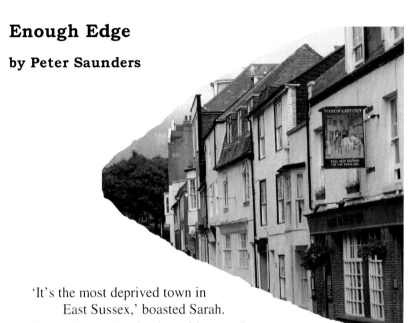

'It's the most deprived town in
    East Sussex,' boasted Sarah.
'Second most deprived seaside town in
the whole country,' added David.
    Some terrible social problems,' said Sarah.
    But Claire looked sceptical.
    'The Old Town is so quaint!' she protested.
    'Twee!' said her husband, from behind his newspaper.
    'St Clement's Church – thirteenth century, was it? And that half-timbered, Tudor pub in George street...'
    'Fake!' interrupted her husband again.
    'The church, or the pub?'
    'The pub,' Jonathon replied. 'The church, so far as one can tell, is genuine. Ye Olde Pumpe House is anything but.'
    Jonathon considered himself an expert on architecture. In fact, Jonathon considered himself an expert on almost everything. Wildlife. Wine and real ale. Literature. Astronomy. Politics. Geology. Jazz. History. Not sport, though. He had, he said, no interest in grown men in shorts chasing around a field in pursuit of a ball. But on almost everything else, he never doubted his own authority.
    'Well anyway,' Claire continued, 'it all looks much too charming to be as deprived as you say. And the antique shops! They're marvellous, and so much cheaper than London.'

'Junk, mostly,' said Jonathon from behind his *Independent on Sunday*, signalling his hitherto unsuspected expertise in *objets d'art*.

Jonathon and Claire were visiting from Camden for the weekend. It had taken more than a year to get them down here. The first date had had to be changed when Jonathon flew to South Africa for an emergency conference on climate change. Then one of their children was suspended from school for dealing cannabis, so they had to cancel again while they negotiated with the headmaster to have him re-admitted. Then a new play came on at the Barbican that received such positive reviews that they just had to go.

But Sarah persevered. Diaries were synchronised, and eventually a free weekend was identified and relevant arrangements made.

They had driven down together on Friday evening, David and Sarah leading in Sarah's Audi, Jonathon and Claire following behind in their brand new, bright red, Porsche 911. The drive down had been a nightmare. The traffic coming out of London was always bad on a Friday night, but a smash on the A21 had closed the road south of Hurst Green, and the detour added almost an hour to the journey. By the time they arrived in Hastings, all the residents' parking spots had gone, and they had to leave both cars up the hill, almost a mile away, and walk back to the house on foot.

Everyone was feeling irritable after that, and nobody was in the mood for the sea food restaurant they had booked, so they cancelled and ordered a Thai takeaway instead. David and Sarah had been forced to admit that the transport links were a major disadvantage of having bought a second home in Hastings.

Once, when Jonathon had had to stay over in town until Saturday, Sarah had driven down alone on the Friday evening, leaving him to follow by train the next day. Never again! The train stopped at places he'd never heard of. Etchingham? Stonegate?? Stations that appeared to be in the middle of fields. That's why they'd gone back to having two cars, and bugger the carbon footprint.

Not that doing the journey by road every weekend was much better. All that single-lane traffic once you got south of Tunbridge Wells, the wearisome traffic jams and repeated diversions. But, as David said, they had the poor transport links to thank for the low property prices. Put Old Town where Brighton is, and they'd have had to pay double for an equivalent place. They felt they'd got themselves a bargain. A roomy, eighteenth century house, sea views from the top bedroom, lots of original features, oodles of character. Even a small garden, which was unusual for Old Town (although they'd still put their names on the waiting list for an allotment.)

They had bought the house just over a year ago. Property prices were slumping and interest rates were low. The banks weren't lending much to anybody, but Sarah had had a legacy from her grandmother and David had just won another lucrative consultancy contract with the Arts Council, so they'd not had a problem raising the cash.

Once they'd decided to buy a weekender, they had done their research thoroughly. They spent the summer checking out all the south coast resorts. Bognor was too depressing; Worthing too dull; Eastbourne too suburban; Brighton too pretentious. But the medieval charm of the Old Town, and its picturesque location sandwiched between two hills and just a minute from the beach, had won them over immediately.

So had the house. It was a probate sale: an old lady, connected with one of the local fishing families, who had lived there all her life.

It had been on the market for three, but they got it for less than two-fifty. The room in which she had been living smelled of urine and liniment and boiled fish. They'd had to spend forty thousand making the house habitable. They had been coming down most weekends ever since.

For years, newspaper property pundits had been saying that Hastings was due for a revival. Now, with the new college opening and the Jerwood Gallery coming to the Stade, the place really could be on the up. They could be sitting on a little gold mine. Not that they'd bought it with investment in mind. And they certainly didn't want floods of Londoners buying up all the houses and changing the character of the town. But it would be nice to have their judgement vindicated by seeing others like them scrabbling to get on the bandwagon.

'Don't be misled by appearances,' said David, picking up the threads of the conversation. 'The town has serious problems. Poverty. Unemployment. Substance abuse.'

'Crime,' added his wife.

'Obesity,' added Jonathon helpfully, from behind his newspaper. 'Judging by those people we saw in the main town when we drove through on Friday night.'

David and Sarah had thrown themselves into the local community from the outset. David had joined the local Labour Party branch. They belonged to the Hastings Old Town Residents' Association. They were members of the Hastings Pier and White Rock Trust, and they had signed petitions and joined demonstrations to help save the pier. They supported the lifeboats, and the local AIDS charities.

They made a point of supporting local businesses, too. They brought their meat and fresh vegetables with them from London each weekend but they always bought their bread from Judges, their cheese from Penbuckles and fresh fish from the shops along Rock-a-Nore. Every Saturday, Sarah bought flowers from Shimizu in the High Street, even though they only stayed down for two nights. They employed a local man to look after the garden, and they had used local builders and decorators to fit the new bathroom, supply the Aga, fix the roof and decorate the lounge.

Sarah and David loved the Old Town and the respite it offered them every weekend from life in the metropolis. But they wanted their friends to appreciate it, too. It was important that they should understand why they had bought a weekend place here, and maybe even feel a bit envious. But Jonathon and Claire seemed less than impressed.

On Saturday, they had taken them on a tour of the Old Town. They started down at Rock-a-Nore, inspecting the net huts, popping into the Fishermen's Museum, and crunching across the shingles to see the fishing boats.

'Biggest beach-based fishing fleet in the country,' said David, as they trudged past the rusting chains and lobster pots towards the boats.

'Not much competition, I'd imagine,' growled Jonathon.

They'd been lucky enough to see one of the boats being winched up the beach. But then a fisherman had shouted and sworn at them, because they'd been standing too close to the taut cable as the caterpillar truck hauled the boat out of the surf. That had slightly soured the experience, but David did his best to laugh it off.

From there they'd gone into David's favourite fish shop, where the proprietor sometimes remembered his name. But an assistant was on duty that morning, and he didn't know who David was. He called him 'Sir.' They still spent nearly thirty pounds on king prawns and mackerel for that evening's meal.

Next, it was window-shopping in George Street. David gave a pound to a beggar with a dog who was sitting on the pavement outside one of the boarded-up shops. Sarah bought a painting of the Old Town, in which you could see their house. Claire bought a postcard.

Then they'd taken the Cliff Railway up to the West Hill and had coffees sitting outside the hilltop café, looking out to sea. It was a beautiful, clear September day. To their right, the chalk cliffs of Eastbourne were clearly visible. A noisy trail of foreign students trudged past, talking German. Nearby, a father was trying to fly his children's kite, but there was insufficient wind to get it airborne. The shrieks of fairground riders wafted up on the thermals and, far below, the sun was glinting on the rippling waves.

David took his jacket off and put on his Revos.

Jonathon complained about his macchiato.

They had lunch in the FILO[*], down on the High Street. Jonathon thought the Crofter's was a bit weak, the Ginger Tom a bit hoppy.

---

[*] The First In Last Out, a Hastings pub and brewery. There is a window in the main bar through which you can see the barrels in this tiny brewery producing their own, specialist brews.

That was followed by a trail through the antique shops checking out old prints, vases, and vinyl albums from the 1960s.

'I can see the attraction,' Jonathon conceded later that evening, as Sarah cleared away the dishes and David brought out the Mataxa Five Star. 'It's a quaint enough place, lots of character. But there's not enough going on for my tastes.'

'There's a good local music scene,' countered David. 'Jazz. Blues. There's musicians play here during the week, then play up in London at weekends. Ronnie Scott's, places like that.'

David wasn't particularly interested in live music, though he would never admit that to his guests. He got bored standing in crowded pubs and clubs where you couldn't get to the bar and the music drowned out any conversation. But he liked to know such things were on offer in the town, and he thought it would impress Jonathon, with his interest in jazz.

'What's the name of that female singer, Sarah, performs at Porter's during the week? Carol something?'

Sarah ignored him. She was talking to Claire.

'There's a lovely little art house cinema in the High Street – The Electric Palace. – Shows foreign language movies, and stuff you don't get at the Odeon. We saw *It's A Wonderful Life* there last Christmas. You get a glass of wine, or coffee…'

'And there's a thriving arts scene,' David broke in. 'Lots of local artists, doing really interesting stuff.'

'And festivals!' persisted Sarah. 'There's always something happening. You just missed the Seafood and Wine Festival. Next month is Hastings Week, with the bonfire and fireworks. Then there's Jack in the Green…'

Jonathon smiled indulgently. David sensed they were protesting too much.

'Yeah, I'm sure it's great,' Jonathon reassured them. 'All I'm saying is, the place is a bit, well, parochial for us.'

'It's very white,' added Claire. 'We've hardly seen any black people since we arrived.'

'It's just a bit too tame for us,' continued Jonathon, as he lit another joint. 'I like a place to have a bit of an edge. I don't sense Hastings has an edge.'

On Sunday morning, they enjoyed a leisurely breakfast, and then they read the Sunday papers over coffee. Sarah suggested they walk off their hangovers by climbing the steps onto the East Hill and going over the cliffs as far as Fairlight, before catching the bus back.

It was another glorious day. But Jonathon got cramp in his leg near the top of the steps, so they had to turn around and come back to the house.

'I think perhaps we should get going,' he said, declining the offer of a light lunch. 'I've got some preparation I need to do, important meeting tomorrow morning.'

'But thanks for a lovely weekend,' smiled Claire. 'It really has been great, hasn't it Jonathon, getting out of London. And you do have a lovely little house here.'

The four of them walked back up the hill to where they had parked the cars on Friday evening; Jonathon was still limping slightly as a result of the cramp attack.

There was Sarah's Audi. But a Ford Focus was now parked in the spot behind, where Jonathon had left the Porsche.

'Where's the car?'

'Some bastard's nicked my bloody car!'

There were engineering works on the Charing Cross line that Sunday. Buses were replacing the trains between Etchingham and Stonegate. It took Jonathon and Claire over four hours to get back to Camden.

Dungeons and Daytrippers –
Memoirs of a Portrait Artist

by Juliette Dodd

Being a portrait artist I meet lots of different and interesting people from all walks of life – some want big ornate pictures, some want small intimate sketches. One of the high points of my year is during Hastings Old Town Carnival Week, when I set up with pencil and sketchbook in hand and draw passing strangers. All sorts come along, locals and day-trippers alike, for a quick ten minute sketch, a souvenir from a seaside town, a visual memory of a happy day. This is the time I can meet and chat with folk. Being an artist is quite a solitary profession and I do love people and their stories, a snippet of their life, capturing a moment in time. I'm able to chat while I work, a skill learnt from my teaching experience: as I demonstrate to the students I'll talk through the process while my hand and eye do the business, like going into auto-pilot mode, where hand and brain are separate, multi-tasking to the extreme.

One memorable occasion happened about six years ago. I was stewarding an Art exhibition at St Mary's-in-the-Castle on a rainy summer's day, a boring but necessary job answering queries and keeping an eye on the exhibits in case they get nicked. Not many people came in during the afternoon, except a few dodging the rain between the New and Old Town. Suddenly a young family burst through the door during an exceptionally ferocious downpour, with them a small child asleep in his buggy, shattered after a day's fun on the beach. He was totally out for the count with a red seaside bucket wedged helmet-like on his head, so I drew this bizarre sleeping child as he was. During Old Town Week last year a lady came up to me and said 'Can you draw my son? You drew him before, when he was little...' As soon as she mentioned the bucket I knew it was the same lad. So now, she has two sketches of her son, this time older, awake and without a bucket – that's the start of a collection!

There are two types of portrait: a truthful one and a flattering one. Depending on who the subject is, this is a totally personal choice and needs to be either discussed or done at the artist's discretion. Women generally prefer the latter for obvious reasons. One example of this situation involved a portly lady who, while we were chatting, told me she'd recently gone through chemotherapy treatment to cure her cancer. She mentioned that her hair, which was now thick, curly and dark brown had before been thin, mousy and straight, and she'd gained quite a bit of weight due to the side effect of the drugs. As I sketched her face I asked if she'd like me to slim her down a bit, to which she replied: 'No thanks, draw me as I am, I'm just lucky to be alive.'

I often take a few years off ladies of a certain age, easily done by omitting the odd line and wrinkle. The result is an instant facelift, less work for me and one satisfied customer.

Perhaps I should charge more for older people as there is a lot going on in their faces, making them a much more interesting subject, compared to the young... a surplus charge for wrinkles

74

maybe, or would that be classed as ageist? Practically speaking, octogenarians take at least five minutes extra time to complete, whereas bearded men could have a discount because there is no need to draw in the lower part of their faces.

Many passers-by bring their beloved pets along, wanting portraits with them both together. There is not much difference between drawing a dog and a person – as long as the eyes, nose and mouth are in right the place, the rest is fur. Old dogs are the best, as they will stay still for a minute or two at least. My experience with a puppy was a real challenge. As it sat on the owner's lap I started the sketch, then it moved, which is not good: after a few moments trying to settle it down again I was now looking at the totally opposite view. Instead of starting again I reversed the image and drew a mirror version, which luckily, aided by its mass of fur, actually looked like the excited young dog in front of me. Now I limit my casual sitters to anyone over five years old (unless they are asleep) and obedient dogs only!

For the more hyperactive young subjects I take photographs to work from. It is amazing to think how the Old Masters actually got very young children to sit still successfully to be painted before the invention of photography – was it from threats, bribery or simply a gobstopper? Nowadays, we have the television, a wonderful aid for me because the child sits glued to the screen for at least an hour, especially if it's a new film, allowing me to draw them uninterrupted.

Working from reference photos is applicable if the subject is too young, too busy or deceased. I prefer working from life, as this gives me the opportunity to get to know the sitter and portray some of their personality. Once, I had a long distance commission from a father to paint his son for a 21st birthday present. I was sent a selection of photographs, showing a rather (I thought) stuck up young fop, dressed in a formal morning suit and holding a rather static, contrived pose. I completed the painting and sent it off, but was not entirely happy with it as I had no idea what he was really like. A few years later I actually met the young man and found he wasn't anything like I'd expected, being a jolly, down to earth fellow and not at all the snobbish poser that came across from his photos and my finished painting. Never judge a book by its cover... but we all do at times.

Occasionally I come across people whose faces are incredibly difficult to draw. They usually have interesting features when animated and moving, but as soon as they are still my likeness of them somehow looses their exuberant personality, becoming more like a cousin or some other close relation. Sometimes you can't win them all, so have another go. There are also the ones who say they never take a good photo – this is where drawing has the upper hand over the camera. I'm usually successful in my portrayal. But of course getting the right lighting plays a big part: shadows show the form of each face and can enhance certain features or hide them.

Often I'm commissioned to paint a portrait that is intended as a surprise gift. With the utmost secrecy, we organise clandestine meetings to discuss content and composition, arrange sittings with the children who are sworn to secrecy, hiding the finished picture behind sofas until the moment of presentation. These pictures are guaranteed to reduce the recipient to tears of emotion (joy I hope!) earning extra brownie points to the giver for their original, thoughtful and totally personal present. I've only ever had one client suspected of having an affair because of this. Luckily all was well after his wife realised the true reason for her husband's odd behaviour! Something to bear in mind is that small children always blab, so a little white lie is permissible to stop them telling all to Mummy and spoiling the surprise.

People are always very curious to see me at work. Some have no idea what is involved in creating a portrait drawing. Like the time a man sat down expecting it to be the same as having a photograph taken. I told him he didn't have to put on a big cheesy smile because after a few minutes that would resemble a rather scary and somewhat manic expression! The golden rules are be natural and, if possible, no teeth. If I do have to draw teeth, I try not to make a prominent feature of them – else they resemble a set of piano keys.

What is a portrait for? Why have a portrait done? In this world of digital cameras and home videos, isn't a portrait outdated and old-fashioned?

This art form goes back to the birth of civilisation, pandering to our human urge to leave something behind when we go, to instil a personal presence, a legacy, an heirloom for future generations. Living Gods, kings, leaders, politicians, and patrons – would they still be remembered now if we had no surviving visual image to put a name to? Portraiture is a time-honoured tradition.

With most photographs, snap-shots, or videos, you simply get a random moment in time. A portrait is suffused with history and emotion: the artist's interaction with their subject, the unique talent and craft involved, the accumulation of time spent creating an original and captivating view of the whole person – not just the surface. A good portrait will add layers of meaning and information never conveyed by modern technology.

There are as many reasons for having a portrait done as there are leaves on a tree. Some want a conversation piece in their home, to some it's a family tradition: personal, formal, fantasy, flattery or simply just for fun.

Now what did I say about a dungeon? Sounds intriguing... but that's another story.

'Juliette Dodd with Carnival Princess' photo © 2009 Alun Sambrook

May Day

by Kay Macmullan

The contrast between the hazy white-blue through the windscreen and the tall dark net sheds in the rear view mirror was stark. Aware that she had to bolster her resolve, Mary tried to see this as an image of what she was leaving behind and what was to come. She had made the decision to leave and had to believe that the way ahead would be brighter than what had gone before.

The morning light and squawking gulls had dragged her out of the peace of sleep into the unknown of the next day. She wondered how she had ended up in this car park at the end of the road – and then realised precisely why she was there. She had kept on driving until there was nowhere else to go. And then, exhausted by fear and bravery, had parked up in the deserted car park and fallen asleep.

With a glance at the black-brown wood behind her, Mary picked up her bag from the passenger seat. Its contents were all that she had brought with her – not having stopped to search through drawers for favourite or even essential items. So her possessions comprised last week's shopping list on the back of an envelope, a couple of pens, a single mint in a screwed up silver paper and a bright, stripy scarf that she had bought the week before. Buying it had been a dry run, a blast of multi-coloured independence, but it had not yet emerged from the bag or been worn, as it was likely to spark another argument about money. Her purse was in there too, but this was of little comfort.

Pulling open the popper, she knew it would contain no more than a couple of notes, the receipts for the scarf and the shopping and a solitary bank card. Maybe she should go straight to the nearest machine and see what could be withdrawn before her absence from home was noticed.

From the direction of the town, Mary heard the primitive sound of drumming, took it as an instruction to follow and opened the car door. Despite this decisive new self, she couldn't relinquish the sensible pang to buy a ticket. Perusal of the notice board and a feel around in the zipped part of her purse revealed that there was enough change to pay for three hours and though unsure what she'd do with such a stretch of time, she fed the coins into the machine and collected her sticky-backed ticket. With this positioned centrally on the inside of the car window, she threaded her way through the busy car park, eventually emerging to see a mass of people at the opposite side of the road.

The volume and an infectious excitement grew as Mary moved towards and then into the crowd. At first, she excused herself politely from the back as if making towards a group of friends or family members. She looked to be the kind of person who wouldn't push in, which strangely gave her the right to do just that. Over the heads in front of her, she could soon see the source of interest. It was as if a forest were making its way down the narrow street – people of all ages dressed in shades of the wood, some decorated with ribbons, some with their hair dyed green, some with foliage forming an elaborate headdress, some a moving mass of leaves. Mary wrapped

79

her arms around her bag in front of her. Part of her wanted to turn around and return to the calm of the seafront, to the seclusion of her car – windows shut, sound closed out – but another part was drawn to the clamour of voices and the rhythm of the drums. Reaching into her bag, she pulled out the scarf and wrapped it around her neck.

Suddenly, her field of vision was filled with green: an oversized face framed by unrestrained, fuzzy grey hair and overgrown whiskers, painted green skin with moss-like foundation dried into the countless smile lines and wrinkles, blue eyes that stood out against their watery white surrounds. The procession seemed a long way away. The hubbub seemed to dissipate. Mary felt she was expected to act, that spectating was no longer enough. She didn't take her eyes off her viridian partner but sensed that all around her were looking in her direction.

As the damp sponge moved rapidly towards her, she pulled back but her reaction was not fast enough and the wet cushion squashed onto her nose. Her hand moved up instinctively to her face. She looked down at the garish colour on her fingers and immediately up again to see the tree man rejoining the procession. She glanced to either side of her, but she was no longer centre of attention. She smeared the green on her fingers onto her cheeks.

The paint on Mary's skin made her feel a part of the parade: picked out, chosen, as if she belonged. She may not have the plunging necklines of some of the girls who wafted past her now, nor the intricate patterns of climbing ivy leaves painted onto exposed flesh, but she attached herself to the throng that was all but wedged between the shop fronts and moved along the street. With no idea where she was going, buoyed along by the colour and the sound, she took part as if she were a local, as if she knew the significance of all that surrounded her.

The foliage and flowers and time passed by in a blur. Mary could no more have said how long she had been in the crowd than where she had travelled to, but the procession appeared to have come to an end within the ruins of a castle. Like flotsam finally dropped by a passing river, Mary found herself devoid of any forward motion. She stood and watched as an untidy clump of twigs was drawn up a flagpole. There were lines of stripy deckchairs and a couple of white marquees. Remembering now that she was alone in a place that she didn't know, she watched the movements of those around her. Some spread out tartan picnic rugs and sat in groups on the ground. Others made their way to a large white marquee positioned next to the crumbling walls of the castle. Her lack of purpose and activity distinguished her from the masses, so Mary followed a group that was walking past. In the muggy heat of the crowded tent, a bar emerged. No one seemed to sense how out of place she felt. Maybe she could even buy herself a drink.

Walking out of the tent, plastic pint glass in hand, Mary made her way towards a stage that was set up in the middle of the grass.

'Bogeys get you?'

Mary turned to see a painted black face smiling at her. A crumpled dark suit and top hat completed his costume.

'Sorry?' Not only was she talking to a chimney sweep, but she had no idea what he had said.

'Bogeys...' he said, pointing to her face. 'got you with their paint.'

'Oh yes.' Mary's usual reaction would be to take the lull that now followed as an opportunity to end the conversation and move away, but she took a gulp of her beer and looked straight into the blackened face. 'I've not been here before. What are the bogeys?'

'Never been to Jack in the Green?' His disbelief was concentrated in his eyes, as the black make-up concealed other facial expression. 'Well, the bogeys, the guys in green, they'll bring Jack onto the stage soon, along with the sides – then they'll sing the anthem.' The chimney sweep stopped at the sight of the blank look on Mary's face.

'Jack? The sides?' she asked.

'Jack in the Green – the walking tree with a crown on his head. He's the Green Man – the spirit of the forest – the winter version. The sides are the Morris dancers.'

Mary nodded and took another drink. The discomfort in talking to a stranger was almost overpowered by the mass of nonsensical information.

82

'Look, here they come.'

The chimney sweep put a familiar hand on Mary's shoulder to point her in the direction of the drummers – the bogeys. The physical contact made Mary flinch but she made the effort not to step away.

On the stage, Jack was surrounded by frantic drumming and Morris Men whirling in a frenetic dance. His leather mask could be seen peering through the foliage that enveloped him. What had seemed jolly began to feel dark and threatening. Mary fought her desire to escape, her engrained discomfort at the threat of imminent violence. She watched, transfixed as the bogeys grabbed at the leaves and branches of the Green Man, dragged them from his body and flung them into the crowd. Imitating others around her, she reached up and caught a clump of leaves as it flew over her head.

Mary looked down at her prize and then up at her chimney sweep.

'What are they doing to him? Why destroy it all?'

'Well, Jack… he's the winter. We destroy him so that summer can begin. You take the leaves home and keep them until the winter solstice. Then you burn them to get rid of the bad spirits.'

Mary looked down at the greenery in her hands. She pulled her new scarf from around her neck and folded it around the leaves. She wondered how she had managed to stumble into just the right place.

A Past Eternity

by Kristina Thurlow (aged 14)

I hummed absent-mindedly to the entrancing pagan melodies dancing about my head, only vaguely aware of my surroundings. From where I sat on a high crumbling wall held up only by the steep, grassy slope leading down to it, I had a clear view over the courtyard, and everything going on, but that didn't much concern me. My mind was elsewhere – well, not exactly. My mind was here, but it was here several centuries ago, some time shortly after the Battle of Hastings.

A soft, buzzing noise soon filled my ears, and I started to feel dizzy. I'm the kind of girl who lets her imagination run away with her, who can visualize mental images so well that they materialize before her eyes, which was exactly what I was unintentionally doing now. As I watched the impossibly graceful dancers spinning about a pole, clutching ribbons, behind my physical vision I saw the high stone walls standing undamaged around me, the whole of the castle, intact.

The inner walls of the courtyard were covered with ancient tapestries and lanterns, and the grassy floor was lined with long, wooden tables, each with low, wooden benches either side. And standing on the centre table was a plump man playing a fiddle, and wearing the strangest of clothes. Dancing around the tables, singing loudly and terribly off-key, all clutching almost-empty beer glasses the size of buckets, were large groups of drunken men, all robed in similar clothes to the musician: coloured bright purples, greens and reds, beer-stained vestments a testament to jolly feasting.

Gradually, the vision grew stronger, as if reality was fading into my mind and my visions were seeping out, as if my sight and my imagination had switched sides. My hearing was going, too. Everything around me was getting quieter, and for a moment I couldn't hear anything.

Slowly, the sound of heavy laughter filled my ears, quietly at first then louder, as if the volume was being turned up on a radio, and

I found it hard to tune in. Soon, I almost had to cover my ears as the shouting echoed through my consciousness, ringing in my ears.

I realised with increasing horror the reality of my situation. I exhaled shakily, noticing I had been holding my breath. I sat quite still, as if a single movement would confirm my rushed assumption.

What was I thinking? I couldn't sit here forever, and if this was real and I hadn't just fallen asleep, then surely someone would have noticed me by now – Hang on, that's it! I was asleep; I had to be. Well, that was okay, though I didn't remember ever falling asleep like that before. In fact, I didn't actually remember falling asleep. How strange.

I came to the conclusion that seeing as I had got there by thinking about it, then surely I could return in the same way? It was worth a try.

I closed my eyes and tried to remember the scene from which I had come. I thought of the ribbon dancers, springing and twirling around a single pole, and of the colourful giant puppets, that towered above my head, making me feel like one would break free and crush me at a moment's notice, and of the endless sea of green cloth, and the green paint that covered every face in sight.

But as hard as I tried, it just wouldn't click. The more I fought to control my concentration, the further it seemed to slip through my fingers. Giving up, I forced myself to open my eyes, sighing with hopeless defeat as I gazed unseeing at the unchanged scenery. My head throbbed from where I'd had my eyes scrunched together so tightly. So that was it. I would just have to sit there until somehow I came up with a solution. Great.

I inhaled deeply, holding it for a long moment before letting go, and leapt off the wall. The first person to notice me in all the confusion was a young servant boy, standing quietly against a back wall. He'd been gazing vaguely in my direction. I hoped for a moment he hadn't noticed me, that perhaps I was invisible to the inhabitants of this... impossible dream. But my hopes quickly vanished as the boy gave a quick sideways glance in case someone was watching, then crept over to me.

"W-what are you doing here?" he sounded nervous, scared even, as if he thought he might take the blame for my unexpected intrusion.

"I'm not exactly sure," I replied, after a slight hesitation.

Should I be speaking to this strange boy who I assumed had lived long before I'd ever existed? Not really.

"Who are you?"

He seemed a little more relaxed in knowing that I hadn't broken in against orders. Or that's how it appeared.

"I'm Phoenix. Phoenix Stone."

Never again did I think of the distant time to which I'd belonged, spending a lifetime with the boy who first laid eyes on me in this eternal past. His name was Edmund, and although he seemed to belong in that ancient world, from the moment he spoke to me, it would seem, he was the only one there who could see me, and I the only one who could see him.

Long did we stay there, in some of the empty chambers of the north tower, taking food from the kitchens without anyone noticing. Years passed, and still we did not seem to age, and nor did time. Within a century, we had the castle to ourselves, with an ever-lasting food stock, and always something new to turn into an adventure. We lived forever, in the time before time, gazing night after night at the ever-changing moon, oblivious to the place from which we had come.

The Spirit of Hastings

by Carol A Ridge

"Hastings, why Hastings? Mum, *why* did you drag me to this boring, shabby little town where nothing ever happens? I'll never settle here and I'm going back to London as soon as I'm eighteen." Chloe had never felt so despondent in all her thirteen years. "Quality of life, oh *yeah!*" she shouted. "I'm going out."

Head bowed and scuffing her trainers along the pavement, she only just managed to dodge a large seagull dropping aimed at her head. Even the local wildlife was out to make her life a misery.

She eventually reached St Leonards Gardens and flopped down on a bench.

"Another rubbish garden," she thought. "I might as well be ninety."

"Hello, my name's Dorothy," a cheerful girl offered, joining Chloe on the bench.

"Hi," mumbled Chloe, wishing the girl far away.

Dorothy didn't leave, but insisted on taking Chloe by the hand and leading her around the gardens. She explained how they had fallen into disrepair and how the hard work and determination of the people of Hastings had enabled them to be restored to their former glory.

Over the weeks, Dorothy appeared regularly and Chloe was beginning to think that maybe she was being stalked by this girl. Hadn't she any friends of her own, that she had to constantly seek out Chloe's company?

Despite these slightly hostile feelings, Chloe began to look forward to their meetings. Dorothy's knowledge of nature and local history was actually very interesting. The girls wandered over the West Hill, exploring every inch. On the East Hill they became prehistoric warrior queens in the hidden encampment constructed by people many ages ago. On they travelled to Fairlight Glen, picking blackberries on the way until their fingers and lips were stained dark blue.

They collected translucent shells from the beach and formed them into amazing patterns in the sand. They chased each other, squealing, across the beach, each threatening to nip the other's neck with discarded crab claws. Life felt good!

On dull days they explored the hilly streets of Hastings, searching for the places where famous people had lived.

Chloe found herself missing Dorothy on the days she failed to appear. One Thursday, there having been no sign of Dorothy, Chloe wandered into the Old Town. St Clement's church with its well-kept garden looked very inviting. Chloe had never been interested in churches when she lived in London. They were for sad people who didn't have a life. To her surprise, she recognised and found that she could name some of the flowers and shrubs growing beside the steps to the heavy, wooden doors. "That's Dorothy and her know-it-all brain," she thought to herself. "I'm picking up things from her."

This made Chloe smile and, in a strange way, feel rather proud.

The door was half-open and Chloe decided to explore this unknown realm. What met her eye were streams of colours filling the interior of the church with light – stained glass windows depicting biblical scenes shone magnificently, mesmerising her with their beauty. She stood staring in awe, gradually and slowly taking in her surroundings. Her gaze alighted on a wooden carving. She couldn't resist running her hand over its smooth surface, marvelling at the skill of the person who could produce such a lovely thing.

Suddenly, she was aware of someone standing behind her. That someone gave a polite cough, making Chloe jump. "Oh no," she thought. "Some old battle-axe is going to tell me off!" She'd heard that church people were snobby and condemned anyone from outside their community.

A middle-aged man with a warm and friendly smile stood behind her and introduced himself as the churchwarden. Chloe listened enthralled as he described the history of St Clement's and the famous artists who had stayed in Hastings. Apparently someone with the exotic name of Dante Gabriel Rossetti had married his sweetheart in this very church.

Chloe pulled a battered paperback book from her bag and placed it in the churchwarden's hands. She had found it in a second hand bookshop and had bought it for a picture it contained called 'Stranded Sheep' by Holman Hunt. The churchwarden pointed out that there was local debate about the location. Was it Lovers' Seat or Ecclesbourne Glen?

"So it was painted here in Hastings!" Chloe exclaimed. "My friend Dorothy and I have been to both of these places. Next time we go I will imagine seeing the artist painting my picture of the sheep."

Chloe's mother couldn't believe the gradual but dramatic changes occurring in her daughter. Her decision to move to Hastings was being confirmed as the right one. The majority of the changes appeared to have been precipitated by the friendship with Dorothy. Chloe never thought to bring her home, but then her London friends had always been described as 'too cool' to bring home to Mum anyway. She hadn't been too happy about some of her daughter's friends and this had been one reason for moving out of the city. The ones Chloe had kept in contact with seemed okay though.

Dorothy appeared less and less as Chloe's interest in her new home increased. Then, one morning, her mother approached her rather apprehensively. "Your father has been in touch after all this time. He asked how you were settling in."

Chloe's mother hadn't mentioned her father since they had left London. The split had been acrimonious, particularly as a woman much younger than her mother had been involved in the break-up. Chloe had thought their silence on the subject was her mother's way of leaving the past behind, never mind Chloe's own wishes. Now, somehow, the motive no longer mattered. Her mother went on…

"…he's doing very well. He has gained promotion. I think his soon-to-be new trophy wife helped – sorry, that sounds rather bitter," she added. "Anyway, it turns out that you have a relative here in Hastings. He had an aunt living in a home nearby."

Chloe heard how she had a great aunt who had moved to the coast late in life. She must have been about sixty-five when she arrived in Hastings. Following twenty-five more years of living independently, she became senile and needed twenty-four-hour care.

"…there is nothing going on in her head. She just sits staring into space and smiling all day. Her mind has completely gone," Chloe's mother explained, smiling a bit awkwardly. It was a pity to inflict this on her daughter but she had promised to take her to visit the old lady. "We won't stay long. Just long enough to say we've visited," she said in a rather pleading tone of voice. "I did promise your father…"

"Okay," Chloe replied without hesitation. "At least if she's happily confused she will probably be pleased to receive visitors."

Chloe and her mother walked up the gently curving drive of the care home with its profusion of roses and neatly trimmed lavender bushes. It had an air of gentility that belonged to times past. Inside, everything appeared clean and bright. Watercolour paintings of local landscapes adorned the walls. Chloe felt rather sad at the sight of elderly people sitting in small groups but failing to interact in any way with each other. They all seemed confused and in their own worlds. The staff were caring, but there didn't seem any point to this existence.

A young care assistant who looked little older than Chloe led them across the lounge to an elderly lady. The woman sat in a chair, neatly dressed and wearing a smile as she stared into the distance.

"This is your great aunt," she said, as she fondly stroked the elderly woman's face.

Chloe crouched down and took her aunt's hand. The woman turned to look into her face. Her eyes lit up suddenly, coming alive as her smile broadened. "Did you ever find the book on Millais?" she enquired in a conspiratorial whisper.

Chloe's eyes widened in shock and disbelief, but she answered, "Yes, and a book on St Leonards Gardens, and also the one on the pre-Raphaelites."

The pair sat holding hands in silent unspoken oneness with each other. The care assistants smiled indulgently when they passed. Chloe's mother could not understand this sudden bond or the meaning of the soft whispers and smiles that passed between these two, so far apart in age. She felt like an outsider, an onlooker. An hour and a half passed and it was time for the residents to be served their midday meal.

Chloe and her mother walked quietly from the building. "You know, you've become a much better person since we moved to Hastings," smiled her mother. "Much more thoughtful. Your new-found interest in art and history baffled me at first, but I am so pleased that your school work reflects you new state of mind. And I must say that the thing that has most surprised me is your affinity with your aunt... the way you pretended to understand her ramblings and whispers shows what a lovely girl you are – to show such empathy."

"I really love my Great Aunt Dorothy," Chloe replied.

What more could she possibly say to her mother? That this was the same Dorothy that had been out and about to welcome her? That this was the Dorothy with whom she had spent long summer days having marvellous adventures, learning new skills and collecting information? In a small child, such a tale would be applauded as imaginative. A thirteen year old could be seen as in need of counselling and professional help.

Chantelle, a friend from London decided to phone her later that evening to talk about life as she lived it. She wanted to commiserate with Chloe about her boring life and maybe tempt her to run away to join her.

"I'm not bored at all," said Chloe. "Hastings is well cool. I'm doing so much. Every week is full of festivals, from Jack in the

Green in May to Bonfire in October, St Leonards Festival and Seafood Festival and loads more in between. The whole town dressed as pirates one week. I can't describe how cool Hastings is…" She paused for breath and quietly said, "Well magic. You could say that the Spirit of Hastings lives."

Chantelle decided that Chloe was well and truly lost to her. "She's turned weird," she informed her friends. "Anyway, I didn't tell her about us joining the most respected gang around. She wouldn't fit in. That spirit of Hastings has got to her."

Peace Garden, Alexandra Park

Memories Adrift

by Pasha Milburn (age 13)

Hastings is a beautiful atmospheric town situated in the South-East by the...

She stops typing, gazes out of the window into the house on the opposite street – a large, lit bay window where an old woman sits, hunched over in a mahogany chair; the colour of the chair itself accentuating the lady's wrinkles and smile lines like a fading map. She lifts her fingers to place them on the keys once again but the words do not come, instead memories, so many memories. They run together like a reel-to-reel film tape, some in black and white or vibrant colour, a few grainy and insignificant, others blurred but clear.

She can see their little timber house like it was just yesterday, the front room looking out onto the square tiles; shiny and polished when it rained, her own bedroom with the quilted bedspread and those tiresome thin walls where secrets were stored and announced. Decades whip past, back to when she was innocently young and smiled at everything; a little older now – eight or nine, and running up the stairs in her new uniform; older still and completing homework into the late night as the moon looked on; as a teenager unhappily staring at herself in the over-sized wall mirror; her first kiss in those woods; making muffins in their tiny kitchen.

She leans her head against the wall, groaning because her head is throbbing at the unwelcome re-emergence of all these buried times. Determined to finish what she has begun, she pushes on but she writes only one word '*sea*' before the clattering of her fingers on the keys reminds her of the crash of oceans waves (and her) and her sibling's noisy feet against the pebbles, smiles wide as melons and cheeks like rosy apples. If she closes her eyes, the smell of salt wafts towards her and imaginary seagulls squawk, spiralling high above her. She reaches out her fingers, a small girl once more, and the sun warms her chilled hands. Cold water makes her gasp but she charges in, splashing her brothers until hair on both sides is matted and stringy with salt. She sits on the pebbles, clad only in her flowered swimming costume and wrapped in a patterned blue towel, easily feeling the sharp imprints of stones on her legs. She's standing suddenly, taller, wearing jeans and a sweatshirt. The sea is violent today, a red flag warning all to beware and she's mesmerised by the furious spitting foam and the golden ball of setting sun illuminating the frothing water. She's the only one out and the sea is an animal performing a dance just for her. She laughs, despite the cold in the air and her breath swirls about her like the sea mist forming on the grey horizon.

It has become a trendy tourist destination and…

 She can't concentrate today; so unlike her. Usually, the journalistic tasks, collecting information and then working from home to produce the finished articles, are such a polished, practical procedure, done with a placid expression on her face. The smells drifting from the nearby shops are mouth-watering. It's early and that lovely bakery has just baked a batch of its delicious olive and tomato ciabatta bread; she really must get some later on and serve it tonight with the fish when Will comes. She smiles at the thought and, through her open window, can hear the voices of a couple of adolescents passing below – "Yeah! So that's what I said, how unfair…mmm, something smells yummy, is it from that shop …"

And their lives move on, sharing only an incomplete fragment with her, like a torn scrap of a love letter drifting in the breeze. She reaches out her slim fingers to push a glass salt bottle aside, and as her fingers brush the smooth surface she remembers eating fish and chips from greasy paper, the fat marking her new shirt, shoving them in her mouth with bare hands, and the small packets of salt that, when sprinkled, would adorn those fat chips like the richest of jewels. She stands up slowly, pushes the wooden chair back, and then in again, so the stout legs clunk against the table. Passing the fridge she takes out a jug of iced tea and pours herself a glass, relishing the numbing coldness of the drink, half-hoping it will wash away these awkward memories that, like the sea, are bringing driftwood with them. She drains the glass, puts it by the sink and walks to her computer again. It is buzzing and sighing like a lost seagull. Hesitantly, she reaches out a hand to pat it, in her head stroking a poor baby gull; helpless eyes, and mangled feather. Feeling foolish, she pulls back her hand and the gull vanishes on a tidal wave of self-doubt. Sitting once more, she begins to type….

Hastings is a beautiful atmospheric town situated in the South-East by the sea. It has now become a trendy tourist destination but it will always remain in my heart as the place where I was brought up, the memories that surround it like the warmness of coffee on a cold day. Speaking of which, the coffee shop on the…

Ballad of the

Lonesome Seagull

by Jamie Ellis (age 14)

Slowly, like the lazy opening of a flower's petals to the emergence of the first glimmers of the morning sun, the seagull awoke. Its first, fundamental action was to extend its wings in a curious imitation of a human shortly after the serenity of sleep. The seagull roused itself, pushing life-vigour into the far corners of its anatomy and animating the still-dozing corners of stubborn flesh. As it completed these opening rituals, the gull dropped from its perch then ascended gracefully into the sea-clear air of Hastings, searching for the entertainment the town always provided.

Wings struggling against the eternal ocean wind, the seagull scrutinised every detail that caught its willing attention. Sharp eyes drifted towards the town centre and chose the congregation of buildings as a suitable vantage point. The indiscriminate architectural designs offered many positions for the various and abundant wildlife. The seagull settled contentedly on such a spot and watched for any signs of food. Stock still, the aerial being was comparable in its restraint to the very buildings that surrounded it. Centuries of time seemed to bear down on it. Finally, eyes honed by instinct sought out a discarded chip packet, obviously the treat of a tourist eager for a mouthful of British seaside tradition. The gull rose, with a powerful, aesthetically beautiful take off action that put to shame any man-made attempts at flight, and landed in front of its reward.

With a brief observation for any danger, it took flight again, drifting on the relentless wind towards the Old Town. There, threadlike twittens hide a world of eccentricity. Legions of miscellaneous buildings cram together, seeking comfort, quarrelling for the eye's attention. Ignoring the clamouring of the belligerent shops and homes below, the seagull flew out to sea, then over the dark, brooding wood of the fishermen's huts, towards the harbour arm; and there the bird stood, erect and proud, amongst the breaking waves.

The bird studied the town from this perspective for a while, taking in every aspect of the view of the small harbour and the rooftops of George Street with its eclectic array of shops and buildings. The gull's primitive mind thought about harassing the regular visitors of the narrow lane, but then its inspection reached the pier, a noble and distinctive image that dominated the coastline like the arrow that felled Harold.

The gull's view took in the whole of Hastings, climbing the east and west hills like a desperate mountaineer, always endeavouring against gravity. Rooves clustered in angry defiance of the sea and time itself. People moved through this beauty of concrete and mortar without appreciating the wonder that lay all about them. They bought and they bartered, socialised and drank, without ever looking. They saw only what they wanted to be there. They manoeuvred themselves regardless of their surroundings, like the unmotivated life of a lesser being.

The seagull, grey-blue markings upon a white undercoat, took in this poignant scene. A mind, small enough to cram into a seagull's skull, thought about how hungry it had become, watching life take place in the town. Ears heard the squawks of its brethren, calling others to join them. Eyes sharp as steel observed a small, antiquated fishing boat ease painfully into the harbour, surrounded by other seagulls. With a squawk to match that of the others, the gull flew from its perch and joined the feast.

People Watching

by Victoria Climpson

Mavis plonked her tray down on her favourite table – the one nearest the window. She often popped into the café when she was in Hastings, and it wasn't just because of the mouthwatering jam doughnuts that they sold here. In fact, she thought, as she struggled to unfasten her coat buttons from their stretched position over her widening girth, she ought to cut down on the doughnuts. The main reason she visited the café was because she enjoyed a spot of people watching.

She picked up her cup of tea and gazed across the rim at the shoppers bustling along the precinct outside. She liked to pretend that she was on an 'obbo', or whatever it was that they did on the police programmes she loved to watch.

There were a lot of people in town today, sales shopping by the look of the bulging carrier bags they were gripping. Several older couples wandered past, some holding hands, and Mavis gazed wistfully at them, wondering how many years they had been together, and whether life had treated them well.

A tall, well-dressed man passed the café, his mobile pressed to his ear. Maybe he was on a mission. Automatically, Mavis looked around for his 'partner in crime'. A young mum was walking the other way, pushing a toddler in a buggy and talking into her phone, too. She glanced at the man as they passed each other. Ah, thought Mavis, they're planning a secret rendezvous, and only I know about it! It gave her a sense of excitement to think that she could create a whole new world, just by watching other people as they lived their lives. Quite often, Mavis counted the number of people talking or texting on their mobiles (twenty-seven was her record), or dreamt up wonderful, mysterious existences for them, based on spies, crime and secret love affairs.

The young woman ended the call to her secret lover, slipped her phone into her pocket and turned to push her buggy towards the café door. Mavis quickly looked down to concentrate on her snack.

She bit into her doughnut, and a smear of jam spurted out onto her chin. Darn! She had forgotten to pick up a paper serviette. Mavis got up and went to fetch one. She sensed several customers looking at her, and felt a little embarrassed. It was one thing watching other people, but quite another to be the centre of attention herself – especially with jam running down her face.

'Is everything okay?' The voice came from Bob, the manager. He was a big man – probably eaten too many of those scrummy doughnuts, thought Mavis. She nodded. He had a very kind face – something Mavis had observed on her many visits to the café.

'Just need a serviette,' she replied, as she grabbed one and scraped it across her sticky mouth.

Bob smiled at her. 'I've seen you in here a lot lately,' he remarked. 'Our cakes must be pretty good.'

Mavis flushed, nodded and quickly returned to her table, face lowered to conceal her embarrassment. Once seated, she stared out of the window and resumed her people watching Surprisingly, there was nobody on a mobile phone. No one was planning secret meetings, or were 007 types on missions. There were just people with shopping bags, weary expressions on their faces, as they trudged towards yet more shops.

Just as Mavis was about to bite into her doughnut again, the mobile phone man came back along the precinct, walking hurriedly and clutching a handbag under his arm. Her detective senses rushing into play, Mavis mentally noted his description and hurried over to where Bob was serving a customer.

'Ring the police!' she demanded. 'There's been a robbery!'

Stunned, Bob picked up the telephone receiver from the counter and handed it to Mavis, who quickly dialled 999. As she gave the description to the operator, several customers in the queue at the counter rushed for the door and began to give chase in the direction of the thief. As they squashed through the doorway, they almost knocked over the young lady with the buggy. She was trying to leave, her toddler clutching his sausage roll in his plump little hands and squirming uncomfortably in his padded seat.

Mavis ended her telephone call to the police, and instinctively went to where the little boy was wriggling in his buggy, crying, his mother trying desperately to head towards the door.

'Don't worry, lovey,' she soothed the child kindly, then suddenly noticed what was causing the problem.

'Stop her, Bob!' Mavis demanded, in her best authoritative voice.

The giant figure of Bob effectively filled the doorway, and two young men from the nearest table grabbed hold of the woman's arms and inelegantly dumped her on a chair. Mavis gently shuffled the toddler in his buggy, revealing a couple of purses that were wedged under the seat of his trousers.

'Police! Can we come in?' The voice came from somewhere just behind Bob – and the day was saved.

It was almost an hour later before normality was restored. The man had been caught, by a youth with an amazing karate kick, as he was crossing the road at the far end of the precinct, heading towards the seafront. The woman had been arrested and had given up the two nappy-flattened purses from the buggy, as well as a stash of mobile phones from her child's changing bag. The police had thanked Mavis for her detective work, and the staff and customers of the café had raised the roof with a rather raucous rendition of "For She's a Jolly Good Fellow."

The excitement gradually abated as the customers finished regaling any newcomers with the hot news of the day and left to continue with their shopping, happy that a couple of thieves were now out of circulation during the sales season. Mavis, feeling rather tired from questions regarding her exquisite sense of observation, returned to her window table where her cup of tea had turned cold and the doughnut was sitting in a congealed mess of jam on its plate.

'Another cuppa – on the house?' Bob's deep voice boomed behind her, and Mavis looked up to see the café manager smiling fondly at her and carrying not one, but two cups of steaming tea.

'It's time for my break,' he said. 'I hope you don't mind, but I thought I'd share it with you.'

Mavis, aged sixty-one and a spinster of the parish, smiled shyly back at the other reason that she spent so much time in this particular Hastings café. And the look in Bob's eyes told her all she needed to know about people watching – in the best possible way.

Talking Up Hastings

by Karen Clow

Here we are in sunny Hastings, it's the place where I grew up
The old town is so quaint with lots of pubs where you can sup
I love this little town, despite its problems and its woes
The people who are true to it are loyal, which clearly shows
So let's not harp on negativity like the drunks who stagger our roads
And gangs of mindless hobos who vandalise our abodes
Let's think about the good stuff. We really have a lot
With places like the castle and the theatre, the White Rock.

Why does everybody moan so about Hastings by the sea?
I have lived here all my life and its done okay by me
Of course we have our pond life like any other town
But I get sick of hearing folk putting our town down
Of course it isn't perfect, we all know that is true
But we have lovely places and there's lots to see and do
To live beside the seaside really is a treat
And the tourists that you chat to really can be sweet
Bank holidays are really fun. The bikers are just great
The atmosphere is buzzing through the day and till really late.

Our parks are truly wonderful especially when in bloom
So for heaven's sake stop moaning. Just leave out all the gloom
Don't harp upon the bad things like the cost to park your car
I agree prices are ridiculous. Our council's gone too far
And our kamikaze seagulls which dive bomb us from on high
They're only hungry birds you know, swooping from the sky
Even when they splatter you as you enjoy your walk
Birds don't have toilets, so it's really not their fault.

Take a stroll along the seafront, buy some seafood in a cup
Then pop in for some bingo. You never know your luck
Grab yourself some fish and chips and eat them from the bag
No doubt you will enjoy them and for stopping you'll be glad
Then maybe just maybe, one day we'll agree
It really ain't so bad living in Hastings by the sea.

104

Pine Cones in the Park

by Christine Barry

Firehills

by Nola McSweeney

Undulating, so elating, where green doth meet the blue
    Sea that's so relentless, it's not as I once knew
Crashing, bashing, smashing this land we want to save
      Eaten by the ebb and flow and swallowed by the wave.

Undulating, so elating to walk across the green
    Where once the Lovers' Seat for many years had been
Now gone to sea and gone to dust, beyond the rocky cave
      Coast eroded, signs foreboded, eaten by the wave.

Undulating, so elating this land that saw my birth
    To walk up there full joy and mirth upon that springy turf
Now the lashing and the thrashing of the sea and all its skills
      Have worn away, another day of life on gold Firehills.

Undulating, so elating the Firehills when alight
    Above the surf, next green o' turf in gold and crimson bright
Awesome sight, nature's light, keeps up the hopeless fight
      Against the sea, that seems to be, that omnipotent might.

Three Poems

by Patricia Halsey

My Soulmate

There is that certain something
intangible yet real
nothing we can speak of
just something lovers feel
for who would ever guess
and how were we to know?
We met on some strange wavelength
and knew that it was so.

Instincts

Low she's crouching, watching, stealthy
    all her senses keen.
Ears laid flat, tail laid low,
    watching in the green.

Now she's poised, and now she jumps
    a flurry there has been.
The prey was caught, and now there's naught
    and so it's time to preen.

Fan Tailed Goldfish

Warm golden amber is my colour, though I am cold within.
See me glide, see me float, watch how prettily I spin.

Through my glass home, strange images, distorting as I view;
weird form, you're closely watching me as I am watching you.

Are you thinking what a beauty, such grace, such charm, I wish
whoever made this ugly being could first have seen a fish.

A Tale of Two People

by Stephanie Morris

'Hello? … Who? … Oh, Betty. What a surprise! You've only just heard? Yes, I lost my Brenda last year … Is it really five years since Bob died? I expect you get lonely, like me … What do I do with myself? Not much – just read the paper and watch television mostly … No, no. It's kind of you to offer, but I need cheering up, not a holiday in the rain in a has-been seaside resort … What? A lovely town …?

A *lively* town? You must be joking … Yes, I'm sure there's a lot to do … Yes … yes … Well, alright then Betty, but just for the week, mind you – and thanks for the offer.'

After I had put the phone down, I wished I hadn't agreed to go back to Hastings. It would bring back sad memories *and* it would be boring. It would be nice to see Betty though. We'd had a good thing going years ago but in the end we both married different people. I sighed. Oh well, it was no good crying over spilt milk.

As the train drew in to Hastings station the following week, the sun was actually shining. Was that Betty over there? After all this time I nearly didn't recognise her. She had put on weight and walked slowly. I felt my few remaining hairs. What would she think when she saw me? The had train stopped so I put on a smile and stepped onto the platform.

'How kind of you to meet the train. You look glowing, Betty.'

She smiled. 'It's the bracing sea air, George.'

'I must say this station looks a bit better than the last time I saw it.'

'You'll find a lot of things have changed around here. I'll show you some of them. Come on, there's a taxi. We'll go to my place first, then you can put your things down. How about a cup of tea?'

Her flat was in the Old Town – or rather, above it. There was a wonderful view of the town and the sea. I put my bag in her tiny spare room and joined her in the kitchen. As we chatted about the old times, between us we drained the pot. We always were good tea drinkers. I looked at her.

'You look as beautiful as ever, Betty. Your lovely hair – platinum blonde, isn't it?'

'White, you mean! You always were a flatterer, George,' she laughed. 'Now, if you agree, we're going to the museum. There's something I want you to see.'

'The museum? What on earth for? I've seen everything in it years ago.'

She smiled – the same, cheeky smile that I had loved, long ago.

'Come on, the bus goes in ten minutes and it stops right outside the museum.'

I was beginning to get a bit irritated. 'Look Betty, if it's all the same to you, I'd rather do something else.'

My words fell on deaf ears and soon she was showing me the photographs of the Bathing Pool in the museum. I glanced at her.

'Do you remember when I dived off the top board?'

There was that cheeky smile again. 'No, I don't,' she said. 'I did see you trembling on the end of the springboard, though.'

She was right – I couldn't help joining in with her laughter. I've never had a head for heights.

Then I followed her to an excellent "Mods and Rockers" display. I'd always wanted a Lambretta like that, but couldn't afford one. Perhaps it was just as well. In 1964 the police rounded up the Mods and Rockers and took them miles into the country. Then they had to walk back!

'There's lots of other interesting exhibits, George. Come on, this way.'

The time had come for me to assert myself.

'It's all very interesting, Betty, but I'd like to go to the seafront and get some of that famous Hastings sea air,' I said, looking sideways at her. 'Very bracing, I expect, especially when there's a gale blowing.'

She chose to ignore my remark. The bus took us down to the seafront and soon we were strolling on the prom.

'When I was a lad I used to walk along here and eye up the girls on the beach.'

'Yes, and I bet you didn't realise that the girls were looking at you. It's just the same for the young people now, except that now they go clubbing. I love to see the young people in the town. They've got such a joy in living.'

It was my turn to laugh. 'Remember us necking in the back row? You were such a flirt in those days…'

Her face went pink. 'There were five cinemas in Hastings and St Leonards, then. There're only two now.'

'Don't try to change the subject, Bets.' The old familiar name was out before I realised it. "Bets" – that used to be my special name for her.

Suddenly, I stopped walking. I couldn't believe my eyes – the state of the pier!

She sighed, and I guessed we were thinking the same thing.

'Yes George, Saturday nights dancing on the pier. That was great.'

'We made a good pair, didn't we?'

'We did indeed.'

We were silent for a while. I sighed.

'Then you got engaged to Bob and I went away. When I heard that you were married, I decided not to come back to Hastings.'

'I'm so glad you did come at last, George.' She paused for a while before she said, 'the pier was closed for safety reasons. But a group of campaigners is working towards saving the pier, so all is not lost.' She squared her shoulders. 'Well, I think that's enough of walking down memory lane. I want to show you Hastings as it is now. Come on. It's not very far to the Old Town. How about freshly cooked chips with local fish?

That made me perk up, I can tell you. As we headed for the Old Town, we passed the Crazy Golf. One of these days I'd have to give Bets a game to show her how it should be played. She was never much good at putting. Needless to say, I kept these thoughts to myself.

'I'm glad the net huts are still here.' As I spoke, rain began slinking down. 'Quick, in here…' I ushered her into a café. It was small and cosy and filled with the aroma of chips, freshly frying. I hadn't had much appetite since Brenda died. It must have been the walk by the sea that made me ravenous. We didn't talk much until we were drinking our coffee.

'That's better. Right then,' I said, stretching my legs out under the table and leaning back. 'Right, tell me all about Hastings, as it is now.'

'Oh George, I couldn't possibly tell you *all* about Hastings – we'd be here all night.'

'Just the best bits, then. Please, Bets.'

I slipped off my shoes. Yes, I was right – she had taken her shoes off. She always did. Under the table my toes traced the curve of her leg. She moved it a little way away.

'Okay,' she said. 'I'll pick out some things. There are clubs and societies for all ages – no-one needs to be lonely in Hastings. I've enrolled for a course at the University Centre, Hastings. I've always wanted to learn more about Creative Writing, and now I can. It's in Havelock Road – so easy to get to. And there are groups for dancing, short-mat bowls, badminton, reading groups – and that's just a start. Oh yes, and the theatres and concerts. Plus, I have a *boring* walk on the sea front most days.'

'Now you're getting at me, Bets! I feel like a fish out of water with all this activity.'

'There's something a bit fishy about that, George.' I could see that she was trying to keep a straight face.

I leaned forward. 'If you were the bait, I'd be hooked.'

We laughed together. I had wanted to say more but she hurried on.

'Right, now I'll go through the year for the main celebrations; the coming of spring is feted with the "Jack in the Green," and…'

'What on earth is that?'

'Don't interrupt, George, or we'll be here all night. There's such a lot that happens in Hastings. Anyway, there are Morris dancers and May Day ceremonies. Oh, and the giants and the fire-eater. It's lively alright.'

I caressed her toes with my foot.

'You're getting at me again,' I said. 'All right, I admit I was wrong. Yes, it all sounds very *lively*.' I smiled at her. 'I'll need someone to show me round though, Bets.'

She never took the hint but rushed on like an incoming tide.

'...then there's the Old Town Week in August. There's a carnival atmosphere – people are really relaxed and happy.'

'Bets, this is very fascinating but I want to speak to you.'

She had moved her leg away again.

'But I haven't even mentioned the St Leonards Festival and Hastings Week and Coastal Currents and...' While she was talking I had been studying her. She was no longer the slim girl of our youth, but then I had to admit that I was pretty bony and knobbly. I was not much of a catch these days. It didn't matter to me how much she had aged – she still had the same old enthusiasm and sense of humour. I began to wonder whether her phone call had been entirely innocent, but that didn't seem to matter now. I took her face in my hands.

'You are still as lovely as ever, Bets.'

'I don't think so, George, but it's nice of you to say so.' She bent down and put her shoes back on. 'Come on,' she said. 'Let's walk back on the prom again. It's stopped raining.'

I hadn't realised how much I had missed the sea – nor remembered how it changed according to the tide, the weather and the light. We wandered slowly back towards the town centre. I noticed St Mary-in-the-Castle, but I didn't want Bets to give me a tour, not just then, so I kept my curiosity to myself. There would be plenty of time for that in the future. The tide had gone out and the sand was sprinkled with gulls.

'Let's go on the beach and paddle, George.' She tugged my reluctant body down onto the beach.

Paddle? I hadn't done that for donkey's years! I rolled up my trousers and let the small waves break over my feet. As the foam bubbled and frothed, I felt the cares of the years dropping from me. And she still had lovely legs!

Later, we strolled back towards her house. The wind was blowing her hair – she looked beautiful. I took her hand. It had begun to rain again, but I didn't care.

Kate's Choice

by Rachel Marsh

"Hastings certainly has a lot of hills!"

"Yeah, it does." I agree. My thighs are starting to ache as I struggle up the steep cliff steps.

"The beach looks amazing from here though. Look at the colour of the sea!" She points downward towards the fat and glittering ribbon of blue. "It reminds me of when I was in the south of Italy last year – although my legs don't half ache from doing this."

"We mustn't grumble," I wheeze. I really should be fitter than this shouldn't I? "We need the exercise," I add, trying to sound enthusiastic and failing. I'm thinking we should've got the lift in the funicular railway. I can feel my face getting redder as I pant and puff my way up the hill. Of course I have forgotten my suncream so I'll probably look like a roasted tomato by the end of the day. What would really cheer me up is a large cream cake in the café up here but I try to suppress the urge. Think thin, not cake! Lucy is ahead of me slightly but she's puffing a bit now as well.

"Blimey, how much further is it, Kate?"

"We're nearly there," I reply.

"So what do you reckon on moving up to London with me then," she asks.

I really don't know what the answer to this is, yet. We finally get to the top, find a spot on the hill and collapse for a rest. Oh, that's

Lucy by the way, my best friend at university. She came down from London this morning to visit me for the day. We've both just completed our first year in English. She lived in London from the start but then she had to. She comes from Leeds so it was impossible for her to make the commute to London every day.

"You know we've got a spare room in our flat now, so what do you think?"

"I'm still considering it," I mumble.

"Surely it must be difficult, commuting from here all the time."

"Well, it's not that bad," I reply. "It's only been three or four days a week; it's not like it was every day."

"This town is pretty though," she smiles.

We both gaze over the view of the town below us. The breeze up here is cool and fresh and the sun is now ducking shyly behind a marshmallow cloud every now and then. We can see rainbow kites soaring and swooping above the hills with happy children holding on tightly to the strings. I can smell the salt in the air from the sea and the grass feels soft underneath me like a thick carpet. We can hear the mysterious language of the seagulls nearby.

"I really need to know today whether you want the room or not," she says apologetically. "I still can't believe that Dana left us in the lurch like that and didn't give us any notice that she was moving out! I hate to rush you but we need to get someone in there quick or else we'll be hit with bills for an empty room and neither me nor Leanne can afford to pay any more than we already are."

"That's okay," I lie. How can I be expected to make this decision so quickly? I've been pondering this since last week when she asked me but I'm really torn! Do I want to live in a small town or the city? The commute to uni has been okay but maybe I *should* leave Hastings now. But then I think, what about my family? My sister has just had a baby and my dad hasn't been well. I like being here for them, you know? I'd miss them even though I know they wouldn't be far away. I'd miss my boyfriend like crazy as well.

"I suppose I *would* like to live there," I say slowly, "but it's like you say, everything is so *expensive* up there. I'll probably be begging on the underground with a tin can within a week!"

"No you wouldn't!" Lucy laughs softly. She looks over at the café. "Shall we get a cake or some ice cream? I don't know about

114

you but I need some calories after that climb. We deserve it, don't we?"

Yes! Great minds think alike. "Sounds like a good suggestion to me." I grin, and we head for the café.

Ten minutes later, we have in front of us hot cups of tea, different flavoured hearty sandwiches and some naughty cream cakes. We tuck in hungrily.

"Jon would still come and see you if you lived there wouldn't he?" Lucy asks me, with a mouthful of cake.

"Yeah, I know he would, it's just…"

"Just what?"

"Well it's not the *same*, is it? I mean, we couldn't be together as often as we are here."

"No, but absence makes the heart grow fonder."

Does it? I'm not sure on that one. In fact, I don't believe it at all. I've seen the room in the flat already. It's small (obviously) and the flat smells of pepperoni and cheese if the wind is blowing from the direction of the nearby pizza parlour on the street corner. I love pizza, don't get me wrong, but I don't want that smell all the time! Lucy and Leanne put up with it though because it's in *London*. The big city! I have to admit I love the idea of living there.

This is a very difficult decision. It's making my brain ache so I decide to concentrate on my fruit scone instead. The fat, juicy currants are bursting with sweetness and the cake surrounding them is light and fluffy. I savour the luxurious taste of thick cream and sweet raspberry jam that I've spread on top of it. I can't eat this elegantly and a dollop of cream gets on my nose. I wipe that off but I fail to notice a sticky blob of jam that has landed on the bottom of my summery yellow top.

"So have you told Jon that you might be moving?"

"Yes, I told him yesterday."

"What did he say?"

"He looked sad but he said he'd stand by me no matter what decision I made and if I went there that he would always come and see me."

"There you are then!" she says triumphantly. "See, it would be okay!"

I'm not convinced. I gulp down the last of my tea.

"Shall we head off then?" I ask.

"Okay," she replies, and we both leave. The sun is hotter now. We're both in jeans and t-shirts and we're boiling up.

"Can we go and sit on the beach for a while before I get my train back?" Lucy pleads.

"Yea, course we can." I answer. Then I notice the jam stain and I groan. I can't cover it up so I tuck that part of my top into my jeans. How embarrassing! A large bee makes a beeline for me and I wave my arms around madly until he's gone. Lucy nearly collapses in hysterics. Guess I can't blame him; I must be like a walking jar of jam to him.

"Going down the steps will be easier than going up," Lucy states cheerfully.

"That's true," I laugh, and we make our way down the hill and into the old town.

The town is busy today with holidaymakers, students and children. It's a Saturday afternoon and the quaint little pubs are already full of relaxed people enjoying their drinks outside. There is a sound of laughter and chatter coming from them with the calls of the seagulls in the background.

We walk down past where the aquarium is and go and sit on the beach. I love the smell of freshly cooked fish as we walk past the stall that cooks it. I don't know what they do to it there but it smells different and my taste buds water every time I come down here. The sea comes into view with a stunning blue glow. Lucy's right; the sea looks like it could be the Mediterranean today and there are little patches of golden sand that toddlers have claimed for playing in. There are a lot more stones than sand though, as anyone in Hastings knows! I struggle to get comfy on them at first, as they're not exactly

116

the most comfortable for the posterior, are they? Lucy doesn't look uncomfortable though.

"Oh, it's so nice here," she sighs happily and stretches her body out so she's lying down. "You're so *lucky* to live near the beach!"

"I suppose I just take it for granted," I say.

It's funny isn't it, sometimes you only appreciate where you live when an outsider points it out to you. It's almost as if I'm seeing the beach for the first time. I love how the sea changes colour constantly. It's more turquoise now that blue. I watch the small waves lapping gently on the shore and I spy a distant ferry on the horizon heading to Calais. I pick up some stones; some are soft and smooth and others have rough patches on them. Each one feels different in my hands. I throw one into the water and it disappears leaving deep ripples in a beautiful circular pattern. The ripples eventually still and suddenly my mind is still as well.

"I'm really sorry, Lucy," I suddenly speak up. "But I don't think I need to move to London yet. I really appreciate you asking me first though, and I hope you find someone else soon."

She looks disappointed but she smiles gently at me.

"That's a shame but I understand. We'll find someone. I just hope we don't get anyone crazy!"

"Good job I'm not moving in then!" We both laugh.

"I'd better start heading back," Lucy says reluctantly. We both get up and we stroll back to Hastings train station. I'm looking forward to telling Jon that I've decided to stay here.

Okay, so maybe I will live in London someday or maybe I'll live in another country after I finish uni, you never know what the future holds, do you? The time may come when I have to leave Hastings. But not just yet. I've decided I'm quite happy where I am for the moment!

Creative Writing at The Bridge

Alison Hill left home (a small Sussex council house) to graduate in Fine Art, Sculpture at Falmouth School of Art in 1988. She made art using manually creative processes and worked as a potter. Before starting her family she was employed for several years in the production team of a Furniture Industry Publisher. She shifted her focus to putting words first, supported by images and design.

Alison said, "I joined a Creative Writing course to learn about writing styles and techniques. The course has been a great outlet for self-expression and an opportunity to meet other people in my community. By using these new writing skills in work, home and study situations I can positively develop my previous experiences."

And this is what happened when Alison started attending a Creative Writing course at The Bridge Community Centre...

1 Jelly View

by Alison Hill

She's an auditory hoover with Earl Grey and broad mid-life buttocks. This is Estelle, relocated on a farmhouse chair located near the stomach of her community, here at the Bridge café. No she doesn't need sugar or nicotine patches. Estelle is a low maintenance, self-regulating unit, devoid of on and off switches and sophisticated specialist filters. Any sudden movements will place her unsteadily on a precipice filled with disordered details that she's programmed to silently suck into the void of her turbo-system. Estelle is constantly adjusting the distances between vast vacuous pauses and incessant dialogue to savour the warmth and aroma of her tea.

"I need this chair love, do you mind? It's busy here on a Tuesday now!"

Estelle identified this as a close range sound and remembered this time to find the eyes belonging to the words seeking a chair. "That's fine, yes," she nodded as wooden legs scraped across the tiles.

"Ta; oh, hold on is it you, just moved into Jelly View?"

More nodding and eye contact is all it takes, thought Estelle.

"Do yer like it round ere? I'm Ben by the way, I live right at the end of Jelly View."

"I'm Estelle, yes mine's the first taste, no I um, it's the first Jelly I mean; the first house on the right, mine's 1 Jelly View."

"Yeah," he smiled as he walked over to his own table, "It's always a wobble at first."

Estelle, being unsure about what he had wobbling, was a-blush with that red signal of a fully operational rudimentary system and quickly returned to her studies. The purpose of today's café visit is to complete last week's Creative Writing homework. Her open notebook states: *Recreate the dialogue in your favourite form such as part of a novel, stage play or a poem.* NOTE: Without visual words what will I submit to the writers' workshop?

INSTRUCTIONS: LOOK AT MY DIAGRAM OF FREDDIE THE FISH.

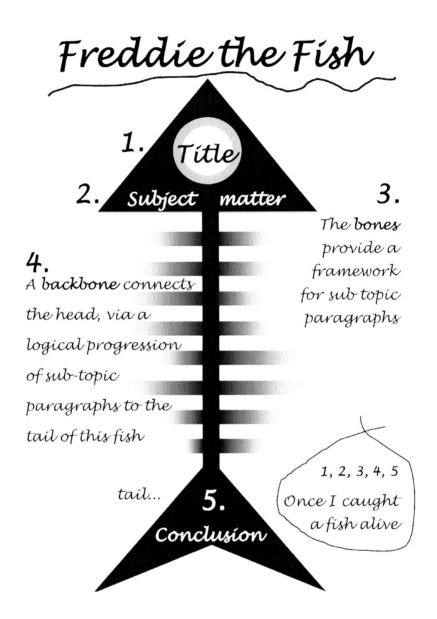

Freddie the Fish

1. Title

2. Subject matter

3. The bones provide a framework for sub topic paragraphs

4. A backbone connects the head, via a logical progression of sub-topic paragraphs to the tail of this fish

tail...

5. Conclusion

1, 2, 3, 4, 5 Once I caught a fish alive

Remember this Fred Fish will tell you how to organise the words. 1, 2, 3, 4, 5 once I caught a fish... Stay focused Estelle, think of gorgeous Freddie's form: his specialist subject, the powerful structure, a coherent meandering journey and that vital passionate conclusion. Devour that dead fish Estelle.

Given the choice between Fred the flesh-less fish and a seductive scent of strawberry jelly now marching through the Bridge café, Estelle begins to write...

I love that smell, the sweetness. My life is an imploding microphone, a grabber of words and snatcher of snippets. (Well OK, that's a bit OTT! For goodness sake I must write something. What am I doing? This is the story of *1 Jelly View goes to her local Café?* It's simple, I must LISTEN and PRESS RECORD...)

"Blackberries; comfort camping; sit down Lawrence; so you've got a new niece; sit down; yes they do; you are the youngest; no I'm not; laughter; I love fish; is he still in hospital; it was late last night; I just carried on; thud, thud, stop that; you really should; you know what I mean; I might be wishing my life away; there's still ten minutes; it was 6.30; oh my gosh, wow; for some reason I know the world record; wow, that is big; you can't be hungry; do you know what I mean; half-past nine; can you leave the students; if anything changes it's not a drama, I can always put pasta on, just let me know; it's OK, I've got a meeting tonight; no it's not open yet; are you tired? It's just like a paradox, I just felt I had to put so much in in order to get anything out; they are very straight forward people, you just know where you are with them; when there's a good framework; that jelly smells fantastic!" STOP.

Estelle draws a line across the page and writes 'RECREATE THE DIALOGUE IN YOUR FAVOURITE FORM.' She looks around and considers who owns which words and wonders if borrowing words means crossing a line or drawing a line. With waves of words washing over her, Estelle wished someone would just throw her one really good line.

Everyone Estelle met said "What's your line?" and her parents had always said "work hard and tow the line." The rest of her family had quite rightly been acknowledged and accredited for their ability to work so hard in all their particular lines. Estelle, whilst proud of this powerful lineage, like a national grid in the sky, remains overwhelmed by all the details, all those little bits that don't fit the pattern. Estelle the hunter hoover, programmed to pick up all the apparently inconsequential quirky bits. Her quest to trap a tangible line of her very own that won't dissolve like jelly between her fingers.

When Estelle first arrived at 1 Jelly View, she quickly learnt of one FORM for words that keeps quivering chaos at bay. Estelle's FAVOURITE literary FORM is the LIST. In Estelle's world the LIST is an accurate compass.

'What do you mean *choose my favourite form; a novel, stage play or poem?* Estelle writes: 'now I'm really lost. I know 1 shopping list, 2 do list, 3 wish list, 4 contact list, 5, 6, 7, 8, 9, 10 just getting through today list. Of course there are affiliated forms, you know like application and feedback forms...'

After pausing to check the café menu, Estelle wonders if she will grasp the creative writer's number one.

She starts a new list:

1. Freddie the F*in fish so F*in E-fish; E-aint? (or does Fred really know the way to go?).
2. There's a delicious smell of strawberry jelly.
3. My favourite form is...

There once was a girl called Estelle,
who hit her head real bad when she fell...

You must always work hard to appreciate the fruits of your labour Estelle. Tonight Estelle celebrates this success. It had taken her team great spirit to hurl the contents of catering trays piled with passionate red jelly across the dance floor. The pulsating disco lights illuminate soft stained globules. This is strawberry jelly, sticking, smearing and sliding. This dense fragrance of Wimbledon and cream is devoid of dignity.

A sober voice of dissent remembers the starving, the waste, the E-numbers. This party is a desperate contest she declares, "what the hell will become of us?"

The roaring rhythm is punctuated by irreverent squeals of delight. A pile of beautiful bodies now devoid of co-ordination and coherent brain function have smacked into this red silky sea. Here we have it... an erotic wrestle, a tragedy, a triumph or travesty?

Estelle returns to the café. She looks at the menu, knowing she must decide. "Yes, that's it, today's special... it's a strawberry trifle."

20th Century Art in Hastings

text by Kay Green, pictures by Katherine Reekie

Bruegal on the Beach © 2010 Katherine Reekie

Hastings is a wonderful and terrible place. It's bung full of music, poetry, art and street-drama, and it's been at war with itself since long before 1066. There's no helping this. Just like good friends who are constantly fighting, if you try to help, they turn on you. Perhaps they're enjoying the battle too much to give it up.

Perhaps it's because of The Stade. There is one set of laws to cover the ownership and access to land, and a different set to cover the same issues in the case of beaches. Where onshore drift causes a build-up of shingle which becomes sufficiently embedded to deserve the name 'land', what you have is what lawyers would probably call an on-going earning opportunity and what everyone else would call outright war. Which may be why our Stade has so often been a frontline in local battles.

The current row could be described as old v new, or east v west, or fishermen v council – but that's all been done to death. I'm going to look upon it as the tragic story of the toilets. I once read a deadly serious article in a Sunday paper which expressed the opinion that you could judge how much a local authority cared about its citizens by studying the quality and availability of public toilets. In this case, I don't know how much of the credit goes to the local authorities and how much to the attendant who demonstrated both pride and imagination in her care of the toilets at the coach park in the old town. I'm talking about the ladies here. I daresay the gents was pretty good too but I'm afraid I'm not equipped to judge.

So when they said they were going to close the coach park on the Stade and pull down the toilets that served it, I was pretty annoyed. Had I been running a stall or a ride on the seafront, I expect I'd have been annoyed about the coach park, but I wasn't. I just thought: "It's all very well to say the toilets will be replaced, but WHEN will they be replaced, and will they be replaced by 24 hour toilets, with lights, and an attendant, and flowers, and hot and cold water and friendly advice on tap for anyone who asks?"

It took some time for it to sink in that they were clearing out that area of the Stade because some big artsy organisation wanted a site for a gallery. I didn't know the name 'Jerwood'. That's a big, outside world thing. I wasn't born in Hastings, but I have enough of a Hastings attitude that I am far more aware of the on-going, hydra-headed battle between traditionalists and modernisers than I am of the larger world of the arts. I could talk for hours about who is allowed to use which bits of the Stade for what purposes. It's far more interesting than the endless arguments over philosophical issues like 'what is art?'

124

It covers things like lifeboats and tourists and toilets and the fishermen's traditions – such as the reason for the tall, thin net shops – you may hear all sorts of fancy ideas about ways of hanging the old nets to dry (the nets are nylon now, and drying isn't such an issue) but if you listen for long enough, you'll hear about a dispute (hundreds of years ago) over rental prices on the beach and the ensuing competition to see just how much workshop space could be built vertically on just how small a bit of shingle. Best of all is the tale of the America Ground – where, hearing about the newly won independence of the United States and, having a convenient stars-and-stripes flag to hand, the fishing community once took matters into their own hands with considerable spirit and declared the beach to be an independent country.

So I wasn't thinking that much about art galleries until, whilst I was organising the reading of the 'Visions of Hastings' competition entries, I met Katherine Reekie. At the time, she was searching in vain for any indication of just what would be *inside* the planned gallery. 'Twentieth century art,' they said – but which twentieth century art? And, as time passes, will we be allowed to have some twenty-first century art as well, or is the gallery to become a period piece in itself? On 27th May 2010, the exhibition of her questions, called 'Art on the Beach' opened at Hastings Arts Forum. I translated the questions into words for the Hastings Observer thusly…

Katherine decided to have a go at putting twentieth century art in Hastings – her exhibition consists of things like Breugel figures on Hastings beach, Picasso fractal beach huts, Matisse's orange people dancing round the net shops, Chagal's fiddler playing to a goat sitting by an RX fishing boat, some Henry Moore rocks at the bottom of the cliffs...

It's really stuck in my mind. Talk about art talking! There was one of that northern woman with the ironing board standing on the West Hill and one of that South American lady with the eyebrows sunbathing by the pier, missing some of her innards, and one of a fisherman's hut with what appeared to be perfectly ordinary fisherman's clutter in it, until the glove hanging behind the door caught my attention and I found myself going over the words of a certain Marilyn Francis poem about De Chirico... and loads more which I recognised but wouldn't have been able to put a name to.

125

Speaking as one who's completely devoid of art education, it's made me realise how many international images I have filed away in my mind. It's a clear statement to Hastings, it says, "you haven't really been thinking about twentieth century art. You've just been having a planning argument. Here's how to start thinking about twentieth century art and whether you want some of it."

Rodin on the Beach © 2010 Katherine Reekie

In my singularly uninformed list, I really should have included the flamey lady walking past the shelter opposite the Mermaid Café. I really liked that picture – I really liked the shelter. I had a very important assignation there once. Actually, it was a tragic, 'Dear Jane' assignation but there you go – it was important – and I was terribly worried that the Jerwood building site would reduce it to rubble.

126

Lautrec on the Beach © 2010 Katherine Reekie

Meanwhile, I have been running a creative writing course on Tuesday mornings out at Ore and who should turn up on my register but the erstwhile lavatory attendant who won the 'Best Loos in the South East' award for the toilets in her care. Fancy her being unemployed… but she's not unemployed, she just hasn't got a job. She's proving to be as valuable, and as startlingly original as a story-weaver as she was as a toilet attendant. Hastings is like that – fizzing with that thing that creates music, stories and pictures but in Hastings, I hesitate to call it 'creativity' or 'the arts' because that sort of talk will have heckles and hackles rising all over. The thing Hastings does doesn't require arts degrees, doesn't like being tidied up and will send you home with an earache if you tell it what to do.

So, like a lot of people in Hastings, I am interested in, but rather wary of, developments on the Stade. Please can we have the fishing fleet and space for the fascinating clutter that is boys ashore at work, space for the tourists and their suppliers, some clean, well-lit and safe, 24-hours-a-day loos, the very-important shelter *and* a gallery that doesn't charge London prices to tell us all about modern art?

Van Gogh on the Beach © 2010 Katherine Reekie

Don't Come to Hastings

by Tom O'Brien

Did you know that the battle of Hastings never took place in Hastings at all?

I certainly didn't, not until I came to live here. And as is your wont when moving to pastures new, little nuggets like this have the habit of placing themselves to the forefront of your store of not-many-people-know-that anecdotes.

The battle took place in Battle – so why isn't it called the battle of Battle? – which, as the seagull flies, is four or five miles distant – give or take a seagull or two. When Harold made his last stand, it was on a grassy knoll in the middle of rolling farmland, and not on the hills overlooking the town. And when invading hordes embarked to do battle with Harold, it is fair to assume that they didn't stop to think where the skirmish was going to take place, though they might now be a bit peeved to learn that they apparently fought it in the wrong place.

All of which is a roundabout way of telling potential visitors that I live in Hastings – and not Battle. A recent blow-in, in fact. From London. Most people trade up. We traded down. Harlesden, Walthamstow, Plumstead, Hastings… progressively trading down until the slowly-drowning millstones of mortgages and high interest rates were released from our sagging shoulders.

And what is wrong with Hastings, you might ask. Nothing. Absolutely nothing. It has low property prices and fresh air. Yes, honest-to-goodness, clean, invigorating fresh air.

I realise now that living in London should have carried a health warning. Beware! Ten million people live in and around these few square hectares of rat-infested, mostly-reclaimed marshland. There's bubonic plague and black death beneath your feet, and the blue skies above are mostly a sickly shade of pale. If you must breathe, please make sure it's not deeply.

And then there's the traffic. Looked at from afar, London seems like one vast lunatic asylum, the lunatics being all the motorists trying to get out. Or is it get in? Traffic now moves at a slower rate through London than it did in the era of the horse-drawn carriage more than a hundred years ago. Did the Wragg stagecoaches travel in convoys like modern buses? Were there five-mile tailbacks at the Lea Bridge turnpike? The bad news is it can only get worse. London streets can only do one thing, and that is eventually seize up. We're almost there now; every day hundreds of miles of motorists slowly going nowhere.

What are the solutions? Build even more roads? Where and how? Tax cars off the roads? Pass Cameron the Stanley knife – he might as well cut his throat now!

Of course there is always public transport. (ha-ha, ha) Anyway, many motorists are snobs when it comes to this. "Happiness is a warm car" was an article in a London paper recently, and it found that many people drove because they found it preferable to sharing a carriage or seat on public transport with people who had a different outlook on life. The snob value of a Lada, eh!

The good news is, you can do like me. Get out. Come to sunny Hastings. Breathe some good air and feel ten years younger. (Honestly, if you could bottle this stuff you could rule the world.)

On second thoughts, don't! You'll all be here then, instead of there. Smog, fumes, traffic-jams, noise…..aaagh!

~~~~ The End ~~~~
~~~~~~~~~~~~
~~~~~~~~~
~~~

That was just a few of the possible

Visions of Hastings

If you would like to see more, please keep an eye on the website for future 'Books Born in Hastings' projects. If you are a writer or an illustrator, or any other kind of lover of words and pictures in Hastings and you have any ideas for events or activities, please get in touch with us.

Earlyworks Press
Creative Media Centre
45 Robertson Street
Hastings
Sussex TN34 1HL

Email: services@earlyworkspress.co.uk

www.earlyworkspress.co.uk